WICCAN SPELLS

Wicca for the Beginner: A Guide in
Wiccan Magic and Witchcraft

HEATHER GARDNER

© **Copyright 2019 Heather Gardner - All rights reserved.**

The content contained within this book may not be reproduced, duplicated or transmitted without direct written permission from the author or the publisher.

Under no circumstances will any blame or legal responsibility be held against the publisher, or author, for any damages, reparation, or monetary loss due to the information contained within this book. Either directly or indirectly.

Legal Notice:

This book is copyright protected. This book is only for personal use. You cannot amend, distribute, sell, use, quote or paraphrase any part, or the content within this book, without the consent of the author or publisher.

Disclaimer Notice:

Please note the information contained within this document is for educational and entertainment purposes only. All effort has been executed to present accurate, up to date, and reliable, complete information. No warranties of any kind are declared or implied. Readers acknowledge that the author is not engaging in the rendering of legal, financial, medical or professional advice. The content within this book has been derived from various sources. Please consult a licensed professional before attempting any techniques outlined in this book.

By reading this document, the reader agrees that under no circumstances is the author responsible for any losses, direct or indirect, which are incurred as a result of the use of information contained within this document, including, but not limited to, — errors, omissions, or inaccuracies.

TABLE OF CONTENTS

INTRODUCTION 1

CHAPTER ONE: FINANCIAL PROSPERITY 6
    SPELLS FOR MONEY 9

CHAPTER TWO: LOVE, RELATIONSHIPS, AND SEX 31
    SPELLS FOR LOVE 33
    FRIENDSHIP AND TRUST SPELLS 64

CHAPTER THREE: HEALTH AND WELLNESS 93
    SPELLS FOR WELLNESS 94
    SPELLS FOR HEALTH 105

CHAPTER FOUR: PROTECTION SPELLS 117
    SPELLS FOR PROTECTION 117

CHAPTER FIVE: MOTIVATION SPELLS 133
    SPELLS TO MOTIVATE YOU 133

CHAPTER SIX: LUCKY SPELLS 150
    SPELLS ABOUT LUCK 150

CHAPTER SEVEN: ALL ABOUT LIFE SPELLS 157

SPELLS FOR SUCCESS.. 157

SPELLS TO MEMORY 171

SPELLS TO FIND THE TRUTH... 175

SPELLS OF FERTILITY 183

CONCLUSION 188

REFERENCES 193

INTRODUCTION

Abracadabra!

Bibbity bobbity boo!

These phrases might be linked to memories of fantastical magic within your mind, and that is great. Everyone loves a good Disney story, but what about the people who do magic without the ever so popular magical chants? Is their magic still valid?

Wicca is a religion that is steeped in ancient witchcraft practices. The religion itself is a fairly modern religion and is not to be confused with witchcraft. Sounds confusing? Here, let me explain.

Just because someone practices witchcraft does not make them Wiccan. In fact, it can be the total opposite. The Wicca religion is a peaceful and harmonious balance of living, and they promote healthy living that is in tune with the divinity of all nature that surrounds you.

In order to begin understanding what Wicca is and what the religion can mean for you, it is also important to understand just what Wicca is not. The reason this is important is that there is a lot of misinformation that exists in the world about Wicca. In an attempt to preserve your relationship to nature as you go through the journey into Wicca, it is crucial that you separate the white noise from the truth of Wicca.

Wicca is not a cult. This is a critical point that you need to understand if you are going to have a relationship with the world as a Wiccan. Also, the practice of witchcraft does not mean you have joined a cult either.

Wicca does not involve worshipping any kind of satanic deity, and it promotes no harm against living animals. So if you see of a spell that requires animal sacrifice, be aware that is not originating from any Wiccan roots. Wiccan spells are not meant to hurt or injure other people in our lives; I will go more in depth about the Wiccan principles later in this book.

Essentially, to become Wiccan means to hold all life in high regard. Since Wiccans can and do practice spell magic, this is what this book will essentially be about. The main goal of this book is to introduce you to beginner's spells and magic that you can use in your everyday life as a Wiccan witch. There are spells that are meant to be performed by covens, but for the purposes of this guide, I will not include them.

I will focus on magic that you can accomplish as an individual. If you are still trying to find your way in the Wicca religion and are still practicing your hand at spells, then this book is definitely what you have been looking for.

To be Wiccan does not necessitate that you have to be a part of a coven. There are quite a few Wiccans that practice their religion and magic on their own. This is what this guide focuses on—your personal journey into the world of Wicca and witchcraft.

Wicca is an amazing journey that heightens your relationship with the world, but like with any religion, it is founded on some basic principles and rules.

During the mid-twentieth century, Gerald Gardner established what is known today as Wicca. Gardner hailed from England, where he claimed that he was a participant in an ancient witch cult. The resulting religion is based on the time that Gardner spent within this coven of witches. Wicca has since evolved from its very first beginnings. Its basis is centered on older pagan traditions and nature beliefs, and it has evolved into a deeply personal relationship between a person and the world they surround themselves in (namely nature).

One of the major rules of Wicca is to do no harm. It is widely known as "An' ye harm none, do as ye will." It might seem a little ambiguous at first, but it is a simple concept to understand. Remember that Wicca is not a religion that is intended to cause harm to others, and so as a beginner, you really need to contemplate what your reasons for becoming Wiccan are. If your intention is to harm another creature or human, then you should reconsider being Wiccan. Essentially, this rule means that you should not bring harm to anyone as everything and everyone is all interconnected.

The second rule that Wiccans follow is "Whatever you do comes back to you times three." Sounds simple enough. And that is because it is simple! Wiccans believe that if you do a good or bad deed, it will come back to you, except by an exponent of three. Of course, this does not work if your good deeds are borne out of a selfish desire.

The rules of Wicca are plain and simple. They follow along with the same basic guidelines as other religions, except that with Wicca your rewards are magnified because of your relationship with nature.

Casting your first spell can seem scary. This is particularly true for those that practice Wicca on their own. It can be nerve-wracking to ensure that you have the right ingredients, that you have the correct words, and that everything is done in order. After all, nobody wants to be in the middle of a spell gone wrong. Do not worry, this is where I come in. I want to help guide you to help give you the confidence to navigate the exciting and wonderful world of Wicca. Remember that you should be focusing on your connection to the nature that surrounds you. I will give you a variety of spells to try; however, you might want to keep a keen eye on protection spells, love spells, and healing spells as these are simple and effective ways of dipping your toes into the world of witchcraft.

While people who practice witchcraft are not always necessarily Wiccan, most Wiccans practice witchcraft. The difference is in the way the witchcraft is practiced. Keep in mind that Wiccan intentions are to do no harm. So if your spell focuses on harm or damage, then you are not following in the Wiccan guidelines.

Now that you understand what Wicca is, where it comes from, and some rules surrounding it, let us delve into those long-awaited spells! You can try them all in your own time, or focus on a few that are relevant to your needs. No matter what you decide, just remind yourself to keep putting out good energy and try to strengthen your connection to nature.

CHAPTER ONE:
FINANCIAL PROSPERITY

Okay, I know we have all thought this: "I wish there were a spell I could use that would just make all my money worries go away."

Or maybe you have this thought: "If only I had a magic wand to erase my money problems."

Well, the good news for you is that I have a solution! No, it is not packaged in a bright-colored wand that you wave around, but there are some spells that you can use in order to secure your money grow.

In the world that we live in, times can be tough. There is nothing wrong with wanting to give yourself financial security. The luck of being a practicing Wiccan is that there are a few spells you can try to ensure that your finances do not look red anytime soon. Now might be a good time to explain that there is more than one way to accomplish a spell. In fact, some spells rely on words where others are herbal. I promise that we will cover all manner of spells within this chapter to ensure that you find the option that best fits you.

Before we dive into these money spells, I first want to cover your altar with you. This is where most of your spells and magic will be conducted. There are always exceptions, but your altar is a sacred place in your home where you can practice your witchcraft.

Your altar can really be any space in your home or nature that you can access. This can take the form of a nightstand, a kitchen table, or even an end table in your entryway. The important part is that you find a place you are comfortable establishing your altar and that works best for you.

Your altar will constantly change depending on your needs. Some witches focus on lunar phases, others focus on the seasons, and still, others keep their altars as consistent as possible. This will come down to a personal choice and what works best for you and your connection to nature.

The four elements are basic requirements needed for your altar. They represent themselves as earth, air, water, and fire. I do have some good news for you though! These elements are all found within nature, and so they are fairly easy to obtain and symbolize on your altar. Let me give you some examples just so you can start building that altar.

Earth can be represented by stones or rocks. Even branches, dried herbs, dried flowers, and soil can illustrate the earth. If you really want to, photos or artwork that depict nature are also suitable.

Fire is usually represented with candles. However, you can use ashes or even pictures of fire or the sun.

Water is depicted with seashells, sea glass, sand, and driftwood, though there are a host of other items, such as water fountains, a cup or bowl of water, and even pictures of the sea that you can use to represent water.

Air might seem tricky at first, but it surrounds us all the time. Some good material to represent air is feathers. Again, you can use pictures or artwork of the clouds, birds, and anything else that can fly.

Your altar can be as simple or as elaborate as you wish. It can be hidden or out in the open. Some people even have altars that are mobile, and they travel with them. Just keep it basic. Remember that you are starting out and that the basics will help you focus. Your altar is a sacred place for you to strengthen your connection to nature, and so treat it as such.

SPELLS FOR MONEY [1]

COINS FOR PROSPERITY

For this spell, you will need the following:

- A small bag. This bag is ideally a drawstring bag. It can be similar to the ones that hold charm bracelets or fine pieces of jewelry.

- Seven blades of grass that have been pulled from patches of grass closest to your home.

- Seven leaves from a flowering plant or bush. It must be the closest bush or plant to your home.

- Seven coins. They can be any type of coin as they will represent your financial security.

Casting directions:

1. Ensure that your altar is set up and available for use. Remember that your altar can be inside your home or outside close to your home.

2. Take the seven coins and place each of them (one at a time) in your bag. With each coin that you place in the bag, visualize yourself receiving money in what

---

[1] All spells in this book have been adapted from: *Spells - Real Magic Spells*. (2019). Retrieved from https://www.spellsofmagic.com/spells.html.

can be called a prosperity miracle. For example, this can be in the appearance of an unexpected refund check or even finding some money.

3. The seven leaves need to be placed one by one in your bag. After each leaf is deposited into your bag, you need to repeat these words:

> *As this leaf has grown, so will my luck and prosperity. I charge this leaf to attract [a desire that you have, for example, a refund check].*

You will attach a different desire to each leaf that you drop into the drawstring bag. It is essential that you are not greedy with this spell. Be practical in your desires.

4. Next, you will place each blade of grass into the drawstring bag. These also need to be done separately and one at a time. After you place each blade in the bag, you need to repeat these words:

> *This blade of grass represents a responsibility. Over the next seven days, I will [and this is where you insert a small act of kindness that you can extend to make someone else feel good].*

So with each blade of grass, you will attach a task to complete that is for unselfish reasons. They can be simple, so do not think you need to go elaborate on each task. It can be as pure as hugging your mother or calling on a friend you have not checked up on recently.

You can do simple things that are intended to make someone else smile. It might be helpful to draw up a list of your commitments so that you do not forget what you have promised to complete.

5. The charm bag should be closed and placed in a location that is close to your front door.

6. The spell is now complete. You must remember to complete the tasks that you promised to in the next seven days. Your spell is now set into motion, and the next few weeks could hold some great financial surprises!

Remember that Wicca is a religion that is not born out of greed and selfishness. So while these spells are meant to bring you financial prosperity and security, keep the rules in mind. What you put out into the world you will get back in spades of three. So follow all the steps of the spell to ensure its success.

ABUNDANCE SPELL

This spell can be applied to more than just financial purposes; it can be for anything that you need or want with abundance. For the reasons of this section, however, we will focus on financial prosperity. This spell uses the invocation of a divinity. You need to make sure that as a Wiccan, you are aligned with a divinity before you invoke them. What does this mean? Simply put, invoking a divinity of abundances, such as Pluto or Dionysus, means that you are calling them to come forth and take place within you.

For this spell, you will need the following:

- One green candle
- A gold ribbon or cord
- A pinch of cornmeal
- A green cloth
- A pinch of wheat
- A pinch of chamomile
- A pinch of cinnamon
- A pinch of lavender
- A pinch of ground ginger
- Two coins

Casting directions:

1. Once you have completed your offerings and prayers, you need to take the green candle, hold it in both hands, and repeat the following words:

   Dear god/goddess of abundance [remember this is where you input the name of your deity],

   To you, I pray,

   Here in this hour, I ask to lend your power.

   Imbue this candle I hold,

   With the great gift of abundance.

   Abundance in [your desire].

   Repeat this chant nine times. Focus on charging the candle with green energy. What is this? While you are chanting, focus on and feel the power emanating from you and into the candle.

2. When you are done chanting, place the candle down and light it. Place your hands in the glow of the candle flame; try not to get too close though. Chant:

   Radiant power of abundance, now give your power,

> *Lend your abundant energy to this sachet craft*
>
> *And empower me as you empower the sachet.*
>
> *Guide my hands properly.*

3. Now you can take the green cloth and place it upon a table or the floor. Take each of the herbs that were mentioned and place it in the center of the green cloth. Also, add your coins into the middle of the cloth. The cloth must be bundled up tightly and wrapped closed with the cord or ribbon. Do not rush through this process. Take your time with tying it.

4. Hold the enclosed bundle in your hand and chant:

   > *Bundled tight in green candlelight,*
   >
   > *Bundle and mixed with a magical twist,*
   >
   > *Bundled in green with a magical sheen,*
   >
   > *Bundled in gold, abundance inside it does hold.*

   This chant needs to be repeated nine times.

5. Place the bundle next to the green candle and move your hands back to within the candle's flame. Say the next chant:

   > *Divine god/goddess, to you I ask*

Gift your gifts to this spell

Imbue this sachet and candle with your gifts

And your divine energy.

This I so ask.

6. Leave the bundle next to the green candle and allow the green candle to continue to burn until there is nothing left of it. Once the candle is done burning, hide the sachet in a safe place in your home. Avoid placing it near windows and doors. If you are in dire need of abundance, four sachets can be made and placed in four opposite corners of your home.

PROSPERITY BATH SPELL

For this spell, you will need the following:

- One green candle
- Three silver coins (they must each be different from the other)
- Salt

Casting directions:

1. On the candle, inscribe the amount of money that you need. Please remember to make this a reasonable amount. Wicca is not a get-rich-quick way of life.

2. Charge your candle and the coins on your altar.

3. Run yourself a bath while they charge. When the bath is ready, add some salt to it and the coins.

4. Place the candle at the foot of your bath.

5. Light the candle and turn off any other lights.

6. Relax in the water. Focus on the candle's flame and visualize yourself receiving the money that you need.

7. Say this chant:

   The green dragon flies over the sea,

   Bringing wealth and prosperity to me.

8. Do not wash yourself in this bath. Simply soak within it. Once your candle is a quarter burned away, you may get out of the bath and dry yourself off.

9. Take the remainder of the candle and remove the coins from the bath. Place these back on your altar and allow the candle to finish burning. Give thanks once all this is done.

BLESSED DOLLAR BILL

For this spell, you will need the following:

- One-dollar bill
- A pencil

Casting directions:

1. This spell focuses on the positive. You take the dollar bill and write on it with the pencil the following words: "May you be blessed with health, wealth, and joy." While writing this out on the dollar bill, it is crucial that you are in a positive and happy emotional state.

2. Take the dollar bill and hide it in the outside world. Put it in a place where someone else will find it. This is imperative in this spell. You can hide it in the first newspaper in a stack or by some popular products in a store. You cannot just drop it where it might appear as an accident. Place the bill intentionally. Try not to be seen as you are placing the bill.

3. As soon as someone sees the dollar bill with the blessing, their day will be touched. Do not stay where you have hidden the bill; it is not your place to see who is blessed with your blessings. You will receive

the money from this act of kindness multiplied in the coming weeks.

BRUSH OF PROTECTION

You can do this spell at least once a week or even daily if you prefer. This spell can work in a multitude of ways. First, it can provide financial security, and secondly, it can provide good luck and safety for you and your family members.

For this spell, you will need the following:

- Toothbrush
- Toothpaste
- Cinnamon powder
- One white candle

Casting directions:

1. Lay your toothbrush and toothpaste next to your sink.
2. Sprinkle the cinnamon powder around the sink in a semicircle. The open end of the circle should be facing you.
3. At the top of the semicircle yet still within the circle, place the candle. Light the candle and close your eyes.

4. You can do this spell during the morning or evening, but you will need to change the chant. In the morning, you will chant:

   With every stroke of this brush,

   I attract more prosperity and luck to this home.

   This energy will follow me wherever I roam.

   Brush be ready, brush be quick

   Attract what I need and make it stick.

   If you are doing this spell in the evening, then you will use:

   With every stroke of this brush,

   I attract security and protective energy to all in this home.

   This energy will follow us wherever we roam.

   Safe from tragedy, heartache, and ill.

   Brush be swift, cleanse all, then be still.

5. If you are doing this in the morning, visualize a specific increase in your prosperity as every day goes by. Imagine your feelings as your prosperity increases. Each brush stroke should intensify the

images that you are feeding yourself of your prosperity.

6. If you are doing the spell in the evening, then with each brush stroke you need to visualize a white light that has an egg-like shape and continues to grow around every living person and animal in your home. Imagine rocks being thrown at you and them, merely bouncing off the protective shield that is enveloping you and your family.

7. The final step when you are done brushing your teeth is to snuff the candle out. It is very important that you do not blow the candle out!

As you can see, this spell can differ greatly in meaning, depending on when you use it. As a general rule of thumb, you use it in the mornings for financial prosperity, and you use it in the evenings for the health and protection of yourself and your family.

MONEY FOR THE STARVING ARTIST

Sometimes when you are a creative mind, it can be harder to earn money than those around us. This happens for several reasons, mainly because art is a harder medium to sell or put a price on. If you fall into this category, this is a great spell for you to master.

For this spell, you will need the following:

- Paper
- Coloring pencils
- Clear quartz crystals
- Black tourmaline crystal
- Fool's gold
- A candle
- Oils of your choice
- Frankincense
- A sharp tool
- Cinnamon
- Basil

Casting directions:

1. Decide on what you want to happen and draw it out. Depending on your process, this can take a few days or a few minutes. If it helps, you can light incense.

2. Take some deep breaths to relax and center yourself. Then call upon the spirits and guardians of air, water, earth, and fire. Take your time and search for their presence. When you feel it, call upon a deity that you are comfortable with.

3. Color in the artwork that you drew. Charge it with energy once it is colored in (remember that you are energy, so you charge it with energy by merely looking at the drawing and sending it energy).

4. Charge the candle with your desire. Tell the candle that it will do as you wish, but no harm should come to anybody else. Roll the candle in the cinnamon and basil. This spell can also be used in two ways. If you are banishing something, roll the candle away from you. However, if you want growth, then roll the candle toward you.

5. Carve what you want onto the candle and dress it in your preferred oil. Lay your drawing out on your altar.

6. Using the crystals, you need to form a triangle around your artwork. It does not matter how big or small the triangle is. Place the candle on top of the artwork that is in the middle of the crystal triangle.

7. Light the candle. If you have certain words that empower you, say them now. Before you end the spell, speak again that no harm will to come to anyone.

8. Thank the spirits and guardians of the elements and the deities that you called upon. Let the candle burn all the way out. You can keep the picture in a place you can easily see to keep instilling positive energy.

PROSPERITY JAR

This spell works alongside the phases of the moon and so is best performed on a night that the moon is full.

For this spell, you will need the following:

- A glass jar with a lid that will close
- Change in the form of quarters, pennies or dimes. Anything works really.
- Lemongrass
- Rosemary
- Basil
- Thyme
- Three cinnamon sticks
- Cloves
- Bay leaves
- Lavender
- Money drawing oil

Casting directions:

1. Your jar can be of any size, and there are no measurements for the herbs that you need to use. Take the jar in your hands and focus positive thoughts and energy into it.

2. Add the cinnamon sticks first to the jar, and then follow it with the herbs.

3. Once the herbs are mixed in, add the coins. Ensure that all these ingredients are thoroughly mixed.

4. Add the money, drawing oil to the mixture of coins and herbs. There are no measurements on the oil, so add as much as you would like.

5. Screw the lid tightly onto the jar once they are all mixed in, and place the jar underneath your bed.

GROWING MINTY MONEY

For this spell, you will need the following:

- Small mint plant
- Quartz crystal
- Waxing moon

Casting directions:

1. Cleanse the quartz before you begin.

2. Place the mint plant somewhere in your home where it can get plenty of sunlight. While you are burying the quartz in the soil, repeat these words:

   I desire good fortune, prosperity, and wealth.

   Grant me my one wish o gods.

3. Nurture the mint plant until it is big and strong. This will attract more money to you.

DEBT BANISHING

This spell also works with the phases of the moon. It is best done with a waning moon.

For this spell, you will need the following:

- Incense
- Purple candle
- Oil of your choice
- Rolled parchment or paper
- Black pen
- A pin
- Unbreakable candle holder

Casting directions:

1. Light your incense and dress the purple candle with your oil. On the parchment or paper, write down all of your debts.

2. On the back of the parchment, draw a banishing pentagram. The way this is drawn will be from the lower left point to the top back to the lower right point and to the top left again. From there to the top right and all the way back to the lower left. You can look up additional videos if you need help.

3. Carve another banishing pentagram with the pin onto the candle. Take your candle holder and place your rolled parchment or paper in the holder. Tighten the candle on top. This needs to be done carefully as the candle will set the paper ablaze eventually.

4. Focus on clearing and banishing your debts. Visualize the happiness and relief that you will feel when your debts are banished. Light the candle now.

5. Take the candle to the east and ask the spirit of air to acknowledge your intentions to be debt-free.

6. Place the candle back in the holder, ensuring that it is in a safe place to burn. Ask that the debt is banished and replaced with prosperity. You can use your own words for this. The candle must burn out completely, but you must be present for this as the paper will catch fire, and you must attend to it.

7. As you do this, you should be aware of the burden of debt lifting. You should not expect your debts to disappear simply, but a path to make them disappear should appear to you. This might occur in the form of an unexpected gift or the opportunity for some extra work. Make sure that you are taking advantage of all the opportunities given to you. Once your debts are cleared, you are honor-bound not to create the same debts again.

GAINING MONEY

This is a spell that is best completed on a Sunday when there is a waxing moon.

For this spell, you will need the following:

- One small green candle
- One flat green stone
- Crushed comfrey leaf
- Fireproof container
- Sharp object to inscribe candle

Casting directions:

1. Inscribe your need on the candle.
2. Place the candle on the flat surface of the stone.
3. Sprinkle the comfrey leave around the green stone.
4. Light the candle and allow it to burn all the way out. While the candle is burning, you need to concentrate on your need.

NEST EGG

Sometimes our goal with money is just to have a little put away for a rainy day. That is just what this spell is for.

For this spell, you will need the following:

- Egg
- Pen
- Paper

Casting directions:

3. Puncture a hole into the bottom of the egg and drain the yolk from it. Cleanse the egg using spring water.
4. On the piece of paper, write a reasonable amount of money that you want as a nest egg.
5. Place this paper inside the egg using the same hole you drained the yolk out of the egg.
6. If you wish, you can decorate the outside of the egg using markers, pens or glitter, and ribbons.
7. Bury your nest egg in your garden. If you do not have a garden, compromise and bury the egg in the soil of one of your potted plants.
8. While you are burying the egg, you need to chant the following words:

I place my nest egg in the earth

Where it will grow to what it is worth

This spell is true it harms no one

As I will it, it is done.

9. Water your nest egg whenever it is possible, Try to use spring water and focus on love and positivity. Visualize that your egg is surrounded by the light of the divine and that it is growing! You will be astounded by what comes your way!

CHAPTER TWO:
LOVE, RELATIONSHIPS, AND SEX

Let us be honest relationships are hard no matter who you are, where you live, or what religion you follow.

This is no different for those that choose to follow the path of Wicca. But there is one crucial difference—you can have an effect on the type of love that you bring, whom you attract, and how you bless your relationship.

When you are diving into the world of Wicca, you learn that Wicca itself symbolizes and embodies love. Trying to attract love into your life can be a risky business, and it really is imperative that you understand lines that should not be crossed before you delve into romantic spells.

You should not cast spells that infringe on another person's free will. What does that mean? Unrequited love cannot be solved with a spell. Remember that what you put into the world comes back to you in threes, so to force someone to love is not what Wicca is about. You need to respect someone's wishes and boundaries if they are not in love with you. If you are positive that your soulmate is marrying the wrong person, then you need to find ways to move on, because a love spell is not going to cure anyone's heartache in this situation.

There are right and wrong ways to cast love spells. Your spells should not be borne out of a selfish or greedy need; in fact, they should come from a place of love itself. Always be introspective. Analyze why you want to do the spell. If you come back with purely selfish reasons, then it is best to leave the spell be.

Visualization is going to be your best friend with your love spells. You need to emit out the energy that you want to attract. You can do this with meditation as well. There is an old saying "Like attracts like," and this is proven to be true. This is why spells can be useful to attract the right partner to you.

With your love spells, you need to be open and receptive to love and romance. This means that you need to invite romance into your life. Okay, I know this might seem impossible sometimes, but if you are doing a love spell, that means that you want to love and to appreciate the love you need to be receptive to it!

There are some great spells that will help you safely find love without bringing bad karma to yourself. Be wary if someone else asks you to do a love spell for them; it can be difficult to understand their intentions, and you do not want to get caught up with bad vibes or karma.

SPELLS FOR LOVE

LOVE SACHET

For this spell, you will need the following:

- A pink drawstring bag or a pink cloth
- Two tablespoons of dried rose petals
- One tablespoon of anise
- One tablespoon of cinnamon
- One small sheet of paper
- A pink or red pen

Casting directions:

1. Draw a symbol with two hearts touching on either the drawstring bag or pink cloth; it depends on what you are using. Take the pen and write down specific qualities that you are looking for in a potential lover on the sheet of paper. Try not to visualize a person. It

is important that you focus on finding a person that embodies the qualities you desire.

2. Place the paper you have written your desires on into the bag and gently add the dried herbs. Visualize these herbs charging the bag and chant the following:

> *Roses, anise, cinnamon, bring me*
>
> *Love, companionship, and all that which I desire.*
>
> *I seek love, and so love I shall find.*
>
> *Love shall be mine.*

Say these words as you place all the herbs inside the pink bag or in the middle of the cloth. Tie the cloth or bag shut after you have added the herbs and said the chant.

3. Take a few moments and visualize on what your objectives are and the type of person that you want (remember not to focus on one specific person). Be patient. This is not an instant get-a-lover spell. It takes time for the universe to match you with someone who has the qualities you are seeking.

ATTRACT A LOVER

For this spell, you will need the following:
- Laurel leaves
- A fire that is dying out

Casting directions:

3. You need to set up a fire and allow it to die down. Sit in front of the fire as it begins to die out and gaze directly into it. Your mind needs to be cleared of all thoughts. Focus on a lover that you hope to attract.

4. Keep a small basket of laurel leaves between your knees. As your gaze remains fixed on the fire, use your left hand to grab a handful of laurel leaves and toss them into the center of the fire.

5. While the leaves burst into flames, repeat this chant:

    Laurel leaves that burn in the fire,

    Draw unto me my heart's desire.

6. Be patient and wait for the fire to die down again. Then repeat the chant as you throw more leaves into the center. Repeat these steps three times, and then let the fire die out.

LOVE UNDER A FULL MOON

This spell needs the moon to be full. The full moon gives this spell the extra push it needs in order to help your spell gain success.

For this spell, you will need the following:

- A circle and the elements (air, water, earth, and fire)
- Moonstones (these amplify the energy of the spell)
- Basil
- Cinnamon
- A pink or red candle
- Paper

Casting directions:

1. This spell requires that you meditate first. It takes a lot of energy, and meditation can help you prepare yourself for the rush of energy you need to channel, as well as make sure that your energy is comprised of good waves.

2. Cast your circle and call upon the elements. Invoke your deity that you associate with love.

3. You need to dress the candles in the basil and cinnamon. As you do this, charge the candle with your intent. Charge it with your desire for love.

4. You need to light the candle and begin visualizing your goal. This can be a visual of you being in the arms of your lover.

5. In order to ensure that your spell has every boost it needs, take the paper, and in red ink, write down your name and your desired lover's name as overlapping one another. Fold the paper toward you.

6. You need to repeat this chant:

   Upon this blessed night,

   I ask that the god/goddess [name] unites two souls

   So that we may find happiness.

   May our romance together warm the hearts of others

   With the power of the herbs and stones,

   So might it be.

7. When the spell is completed, you must leave an offering for your chosen deity.

BEAUTY FOUND WITHIN AND OUT

Have you ever heard the saying "Beauty is in the eye of the beholder"?

Well, this is true. But sometimes, we want the beholder to appreciate our beauty that we hold within us. This spell is designed to bring out your inner and outer beauty so that they can shine for others to see.

For this spell, you will need the following:

- A dark area
- A small bowl
- Water
- Essential oils of your choosing
- A pink candle
- Matches
- Unscented lotion

Casting directions:

1. Once you have found an ideal space that is dark or that you have made dark, fill your bowl with water and light your candle.

2. Relax your body and nerves. Place two drops of your oil into the water. Mix the water and oil with a spoon or your finger for about five seconds. It is beneficial to use your fingers simply.

3. Dip your fingers into the mixture of oil and water and spread the water mixture over your face gently. Do this as if you were applying face cream. Be careful to avoid direct contact with your eyes.

4. As you are rubbing the water and oil onto your face, repeat these words:

    Precious beauty from within,

    Let me feel you upon my skin.

    Beautiful inside and out I long to be,

    This is my request so might it be.

5. You need to repeat this chant five times as you are lining your face with the water and oil. Once you are done, you can rinse your face off with clean water.

6. Rub the unscented lotion into your face. This spell should be done at least once a week to feel its full effects.

SIMPLE LOVE

You need to be careful with this spell; it is to make anyone fall in love with you. So be aware as you do it and make sure that your intentions are true.

For this spell, you will need the following:

- Fresh rose petals
- Some blood from the one you love or a lock of their hair
- A red or pink candle

Casting directions:

1. Light the candle, and send it positive energy. In the flame of the candle, burn the fresh rose petals. As you burn the petals, drop the blood or the lock of hair onto the burning petals. Repeat this chant as you burn the petals:

    Love is life.

    Love can change.

    Find the one who is for me.

    Make him/her love me for all eternity.

    As you complete this chant, scream as loud as you can the following words:

    So might it be!

LOVE POTION #9

This spell is fairly simple, but it can become complex, especially if you have the wrong intentions. You need to use this spell ethically as it is supposed to make someone fall in love with you. After all, it is a love potion. Because this love potion has a lot of symbolism, I am going to indicate what each ingredient symbolizes.

For this spell, you will need the following:

- Basil—symbolizes love
- Thyme—symbolizes affection
- Patchouli—symbolizes passion
- Lavender—symbolizes devotion
- Yarrow—symbolizes everlasting love
- Oregano—symbolizes joy
- Fennel—symbolizes flattery
- Cinnamon—symbolizes the spice and passion of love
- Vanilla—symbolizes the sweetness and kindness of love
- Two jasmine flowers—symbolizes love
- Hot water
- Paper

- A book that represents a love story
- A pink or red marker
- An item of jewelry or an accessory that you wear every day
- An item that represents you
- An item that reminds you of (or represents) the lover you want to use the potion on
- A container that means something to you

Casting directions:

1. All the herbs, except for one of the jasmine flowers, needs to be cut into small pieces.

2. Place the chopped-up herbs in hot water and let them steep for three minutes.

3. Add the vanilla and cinnamon. Stir the mixture for three minutes.

4. Take the item that you wear every day and dip it into the water while you say this chant:

    I love him, and he loves me.

    We shall be together for eternity.

    I love him, and he loves me.

    We are perfect together, so might it be.

If you need to change the gender specification in the spell, you can most certainly do so without affecting it.

5. Repeat the previous step with the item that represents your love. Add the jasmine flower that you saved earlier to the water during this step as well. If the item you are using is susceptible to water, you can waterproof it before dipping it in hot water. Remember to repeat the chant as you dip your lover's item into the water.

   I love him, and he loves me.

   We shall be together for eternity.

   I love him, and he loves me.

   We are perfect together, so might it be.

6. Now, remove all the items from the water. Take the whole jasmine flower and place it in the container you brought. Hide this container. You want to preserve the flower because if it is destroyed, then your spell will be broken.

7. Dip your finger into the potion and apply it to your wrists, like you would with a perfume.

8. On the front of the paper, write your lover's name. On the back of the paper, write the chant that you used

as you dipped the items into the potion. Hide this paper between your favorite pages of the love book.

9. Pour the remainder of the potion outside on a patch of dirt. This is a sacrifice to the earth who will help the potion have an effect.

I am going to re-stress how important it is to be careful with the use of this love spell. You need to ensure that your lover reciprocates your feelings and you are doing this to strengthen that bond. Never take away someone's free will.

A LOVE THAT LASTS FOR ETERNITY

For this spell, you will need the following:
- Rose petals
- Lipstick
- A piece of paper
- A red pen
- Rose incense
- Rose quartz
- Strong emotions/feelings for your love

Casting directions:

1. Take a seat and relax. Burn the rose incense. Your rose quartz should be placed and kept next to your paper, and this paper should be in front of you.

2. Write your love's full name on the piece of paper. Then you will drop the rose petals on top of this paper as you chant:

    Goddess of love, I call upon thee

    To guide my success to the one I truly adore.

    Please make [name of your love] my partner,

    And may we love each other for an eternity.

    This is my wish, so might it be!

3. Fold the paper with the petals still in it. Kiss this paper once it is folded, leaving marks with your lipstick.

4. Bury the paper under a rose to ensure that it works.

THE ONE

For this spell, you will need the following:

- One yard of red yarn
- One yard of white yarn
- Blank paper
- Black marker or pen
- Two cinnamon sticks
- A small red candle

Casting directions:

1. Cast your circle. Place your items for the spell in the middle of the circle.

2. On the paper, write a list of specific qualities that you want the person you envision to have. Wrap this paper with your list of qualities around the cinnamon sticks. The yarn then gets wrapped and tied around the paper.

3. Ask a goddess of love to bring your soulmate to you.

4. Light your candle and visualize meeting your love face-to-face. Never lose faith; it is important to keep faith up in order for this spell to work.

BEDTIME ATTRACTION

This spell is best done on the night of a full moon as the moonlight strengthens the power of the spell. Use it wisely to call someone you love toward you.

For this spell, you will need the following:

- A red or pink pen
- Paper

Casting directions:

1. On the paper, write out your love's full name. Draw a heart around the name of your love. Directly under the heart, write these words: "Will fall in love with — —" To complete the sentence, add your full name. Draw more hearts to surround both your names.

2. Fold the paper toward you three times. Pull the paper toward your chest as you visualize the person you love loving you in return. As you think about this person, hold the paper out into the moonlight. Keep their mental picture alive in your mind when you do this.

3. Kiss the paper. Keep it by your lips, but barely touch the paper with your lips after you kiss it.

4. With the paper lightly brushing against your lip, close your eyes and chant:

Let my love fall for me.

Let them want to be with me.

We will love each other for eternity.

This is my will, so might it be.

5. As the spell is complete, thank the goddess of love. Place the paper underneath your pillow before you go to sleep. Visualize the object of your love every night before you go to sleep.

MADLY IN LOVE

I do not want to sound like a Debbie Downer. In fact, I want the exact opposite! I want you to flourish in your journey with Wicca. But when it comes to love, I do feel like warnings are important, especially for spells as potent as this one. This is more than just a simple love spell and is often used to prompt for marriage. This spell's purpose is to heighten feelings of love, but when misused, it can have serious consequences. Always evaluate what your intentions are before completing a love spell like this.

For this spell, you will need the following:

- Orange juice
- Spring water
- Rosewater

- Nutmeg
- One pink candle

Casting directions:

1. Blend the orange juice, spring water, rosewater, and nutmeg into a drink.

2. Light the candle and place your potion next to the candle. Once you have done this, repeat this enchantment:

    Oh, Goddess Aphrodite,

    This is the one for me.

    Now help him to see.

    His heart belongs to me.

3. Split this potion between yourself and your love. Drink the entire cup of potion and stare into each other's eyes. This solidifies the bond that the potion will create.

TRUE LOVE

Sometimes knowing who your true love is can be challenging. Thankfully, for those in the Wiccan world, there are spells we can use to find out if our lover is really our true love.

For this spell, you will need the following:
- one pink candle
- two white candles
- paper with your lover's name on it
- a bowl of water

Casting directions:
1. Light all three candles and line them up in this order: white, pink, and white.
2. Put the bowl of water right in front of the candles and hold up the paper with your love's name on it. Say this enchantment ten times:

    To find my love, I ask the angels above,

    Help me on my quest to find the love that I request.

    Help me find the one I need,

    Who will help me through hard times and greed.

3. As you are on the last repetition of this enchantment, set the paper alight by using the pink candle in the middle. As the paper is burning, drop it into the bowl of water.

SPELLS ABOUT SEX AND EROTIC FEELINGS

Yes! The long-awaited spell section! We are all human, and as humans, we have basic sexual needs. There is no sense in denying this. It is true. And you should embrace your sexual nature!

Sex spells can be used for a myriad of different situations, but the main reason they are needed? To revive the spark that has died or to incite feelings of passion among lovers. Keep reading, and you might find a spell or two that you want to practice with a lover!

BURNING DESIRE

Be cautious with this one as it causes the lover to crave you with a burning desire. You might just get more than you bargained for.

For this spell, you will need the following:

- One pink candle
- One red candle
- One bottle of apple blossom oil
- A piece of parchment paper
- Red pen
- One envelope

Casting directions:

1. Anoint both candles with the apple blossom oil. Light both of the candles and place the pink candle on your left side and the red candle on your right side. Sit in the middle of the floor between the candles. Visualize what you hope to achieve with this spell.

2. As you visualize your desires, chant these words:

    I want you to want me,

    I want you to need me,

I want you to desire me,

I want you to lust after me.

I want you to see that we were meant to be.

I want lust to overflow your body.

In this night of passion, only you can lust and desire for me.

This is my will, so might it be.

Chant it five times, and then blow out the candles.

3. On the parchment paper, use the red ink to write down your lover's name. Write down all your desires beneath this. Include what you want the situation between you and your lover to develop into.

4. Pour the wax from the red candle all over your lover's name.

5. Pour the wax from the pink candle all over your written desires.

6. Once the wax is dry, fold the parchment and seal it in the envelope. Carry the envelope with you wherever you go until your lover approaches you.

7. Once you have had your night of passion and fulfillment, you can discard the envelope.

APHRODITE'S JAR OF LOVE

For this spell, you will need the following:

- Red or pink paper
- Envelope
- Red, white, or pink candle
- Matches
- Lipstick
- ChapStick
- Rose petals
- A cinnamon stick
- Lavender petals
- A vanilla bean (alternatively you can use ¼ teaspoon of vanilla extract)
- An item that you hold of value
- An item of value to your loved one
- A jar
- Honey
- An offering for Aphrodite. This can be an orange, orange blossoms, roses, or even shiny stones.

Casting directions:

1. Draw a pentagram and place the empty jar in the center of the pentagram.

2. Tear up the rose petals and place them in the jar. Add the vanilla to the jar. Crumble the cinnamon stick into smaller pieces, and add them with the lavender to the jar. Also, place the small items of value for both you and your lover into the jar. Place your offering to Aphrodite in the jar as well.

3. Light the candle. On the piece of paper, write your name on the top with lipstick or ChapStick. If you are a woman, you will use lipstick. If you are male, you will use ChapStick. In the center of the paper, write: "I call upon the Goddess Aphrodite. Please, I wish to bring my lover to me with open arms. Make him mine and mine alone. Let him open his eyes and think of me as he awakens from his sleep. Show him I am all he needs and that I have proved myself to him. Make my love come to me. This is my wish, so might it be."

4. Seal this spell within the envelope and drip wax over the envelope to seal it. Add this to the jar. Add the honey into the jar until you have filled the jar up. Seal it tightly and drip a drop or two of the wax onto the jar's lid.

5. Store the jar somewhere safe in your home.

DESIRED HEART

For this spell, you will need the following:

- A satin bag
- 1–3 cinnamon sticks
- One tablespoon of vanilla extract
- One hazelnut
- One carton of matches
- Red yarn
- A small card
- One chocolate bar

Casting directions:

1. You need to keep in mind what chocolate you are using. Try to use a bar of pure chocolate that is 50 percent or more chocolate if you are looking for true love. If what you are looking for are lust and desire, then your regular Hershey's bar will work just fine. Place the chocolate in the satin bag.

2. Shave the cinnamon sticks and place those in the bag with the chocolate. The cinnamon symbolizes the heat in your relationship.

3. Vanilla extract is crucial. You need to pour enough in the bag to ensure that it will burn, but be careful not to oversaturate the bag with the extract.

4. Add your hazel into the bag.

5. On a small card, write what traits and qualities you want in your desired partner. Try not to use names or have a specific person in mind. Once you have written the traits that you want down, add the card to your satin bag.

6. Light a match and drop it into the bag. Quickly use the yarn and tie the bag shut. As the bag is burning, you must chant this:

> *Venus and Cupid, with your power and might*
>
> *I enchant them into this bag burning bright*
>
> *Let my fantasies and desires for love cease to be an illusion*
>
> *And may they change into a reality*
>
> *From the fire in my heart*
>
> *Spread like wildfire the flames of love, ignite.*

SEXUAL ENHANCEMENT

This spell is used to help out a lover who needs an increase in their libido. Please always make sure to get consent as you do not want to impede on anyone's free will.

For this spell, you will need the following:

- A picture of your lover
- Incense
- One red candle

Casting directions:

1. Burn any incense that you choose.//
2. Light the red candle. And as you calm yourself, focus on the picture of your lover as you chant:

   Goddess [input the name of the deity you are calling upon], grant my request

   Goddess [input name of deity], here my plea

   Open the floodgates of desire in the person for whom my heart desires.

   Let them feel the heat, oh Goddess, of my body warm and sweet.

3. Using the flame of the red candle, burn the picture you are holding of your lover.

FIERY LUST

For this spell, you will need the following:

- A red candle
- Paper
- pen

Casting directions:

1. Write your lover's name on the paper. Make sure that your thoughts surround your lover during this enchantment.

2. Light the candle. Hold the paper above the candle, setting the paper alight as you chant:

   Let thoughts of [lover's name] abound

   By this firelight, lust surround

   Their gentle smile and smoldering gaze

   Make them alluring in all ways

   Make their spirit yearn for mine

   Hunger for me all the time

   Let their body crave just me

   By my words so, might it be.

LUSTY TEA

For this spell, you will need the following:

- Water
- Source of heat (such as a stove)
- Knife
- Lighter
- Two pink candles
- Green tea leaves
- Korean ginseng
- Licorice root
- Dried rosemary

Casting directions:

1. With the lighter, light both candles and set one on each side of you.

2. Slice or grate the licorice root and ginseng into pieces that can be steeped in a tea.

3. Mix the ginseng, licorice root, rosemary, and green tea leaves altogether.

4. Fill a mug with water that you have heated. Using a tea strainer, steep the green tea leaf mixture into the water for two minutes.

5. Drink the tea once you have steeped it and make sure to take deep breaths of the aroma the tea emits. This should increase lusty desire.

LUSTY BATH TIME

For this spell, you will need the following:
- One cup Epsom salt
- 2/3 cup table salt
- 1/3 cup baking soda
- 14 drops of orange oil
- 14 drops of lime oil
- 10 drops of rosemary oil
- 8 drops of cinnamon oil
- 9 small red candles

Casting directions:
1. Place the candles around the bathtub in a half circle.
2. Mix all the other ingredients together and spread it into a tub full of warm or hot water.
3. As you bathe, light the candles that you set out and relax.

PASSION UNDER COVERS

For this spell, you will need the following:

- One red candle
- Musk oil
- Musk incense
- Red satin

Casting directions:

1. Write your lover's name on the red candle.

2. Using the musk oil, stroke the candle nine times. Then pass the candle through the smoke of the musk incense.

3. Once a day, every day, light the candle and allow it to burn for just half an inch. As you light it, visualize a building passion between you and your loved one.

4. Once the candle has burnt out completely, wrap the remains in red satin. Place this underneath your pillow for a whole month.

LOVE OIL

For this spell, you will need the following:
- Five red rose petals that are dried
- One yarrow flower
- One sprig of lavender
- One teaspoon of lotus oil
- One red or pink candle
- One mortar and pestle
- ½ teaspoon of rose oil
- ½ teaspoon of lavender oil
- ½ teaspoon of cinnamon
- ½ teaspoon of rose salt

Casting directions:
1. Make this oil on a sunny day. Mix all the dry ingredients in the mortar.
2. Place the red candle directly in front of you and light it. Now you can add the oils to the dry mixture.
3. Dip your fingers into the oil mixture and allow your energy to flow into the oil. Visualize what the oil will be able to do for you.

4. You can preserve the oil and dab a little bit of it around your wrists each day. It will make your inner beauty shine and bring you love.

FRIENDSHIP AND TRUST SPELLS

No man wants to be a lonely island. That is true for Wiccans as well. We all benefit from a healthy friendship, but sometimes it can be hard to build bridges of trust and even harder to put ourselves out there in order to find new friends.

If you are new to Wicca, you might be nervous about making friends in the Wiccan community or even friends who you are afraid will not understand the Wiccan community. It is okay to be nervous, but I have some good news for you. There is a spell for everything, and even on matters of friendship, Wicca can help you.

FINDING FRIENDS

For this spell, you will need the following:

- Dirt
- Sweet pea flower petals
- A pink candle
- Plastic bag

- Lemon peelings
- Rosemary

Casting directions:

1. Open the plastic bag, and put your sweet pea petals inside the bag. While you do this, visualize a new friendship being planted.

2. Cover the petals with the dirt and visualize a new friendship growing from this.

3. Gently put your lemon peelings on top of the dirt, and then sprinkle the rosemary over the lemon peelings. Close the bag carefully while saying the following chant:

   I open myself up for a new friendship, allowing it to grow as long as it needs.

   I request the gods and goddesses' helping hands, leading me to the true friendship.

   While this candle is their guiding light,

   I will be looking for their sight.

   This is my will, this is my plea, so might it be.

4. Light the candle while doing the chant and place the lit candle on top of the bag. If needed, place a jar lid on top of the plastic bag, then put your candle on that for more balance.

5. Allow the candle to go out on its own, but pay attention to the smoke of the candle fire. If it is needed, snuff out the candle.

6. Once the candle has burned all the way down and it has gone out on its own, you should bury the bag outside. If you decide not to bury it, you should put it in a safe place where it will not be disturbed in your home.

REVIVING OLD FRIENDSHIPS

For this spell, you will need the following:
- A white candle
- Sandalwood oil
- Sandalwood incense
- Photo of the friend
- Glass of water
- Salt

Casting directions:

1. Dress the candle with the oil, and then light the white candle and the incense.

2. Place the picture of your friend on your altar. Put two heaping tablespoons of salt into your right palm.

3. Allow a small amount of salt trickle into the glass of water while making the sign of the equal-armed cross of the elements. Make this cross three times.

4. As you make the cross, speak aloud, "Call me," three times.

5. Then set the glass on the altar and speak aloud, "Get in touch with me, please."

6. Your friend should have made contact with you by the time the water has evaporated from the glass.

FRIENDSHIP CAULDRON SPELL

For this spell, you will need the following:
- One cauldron with water in it
- A piece of paper
- A red candle

Casting directions:

1. Write down the name of the friend with whom you want a better relationship with. This is best done during a full moon so that you have the most energy. Chant the lines below:

   Fire burns red as does my mind for your friendship,

   Together we can brave any hardship.

   With each other by our side,

   Our hearts will always stay allied.

   I enjoy your visits most of all,

   Of our first days, I will always recall.

2. After repeating these lines, burn the small piece of paper with the flame from the red candle. As the paper burns, drop it into the cauldron. Let it burn until it stops on its own. Afterward, you should pour the cauldron water and remains from the paper onto the ground within view of the moon.

BINDING FRIENDSHIP

This spell is meant to maintain loyalty within a friendship. For this spell, you will need the following:

- One yellow candle
- An item that is personal to the friend
- An item that is personal to you
- A picture of you and the friend together
- A green box
- Red thread

Casting directions:

1. Cast a circle and sweep the floor with a besom (a broom that is made from twigs and wound together around a stick).

2. Visualize for a few moments what you want and how things will be when you finish the spell. Before lighting the candle, inscribe it with the astrological symbol of Jupiter (for prosperity) and Saturn (for binding).

3. Light the candle and chant:

    Friendship eternal, true and steadfast
    I shall have thee now at last.

4. Bind the personal item from you and from your friend together with the red thread. While you are doing this, chant:

   *You and I bound together in friendship
   and trust now and forever!*

   Then tie the thread and make a secure knot around the items. Keep visualizing your friendship.

5. Now take the picture hold it in your hands. Send energy into it as you chant:

   *More than brothers/sisters we are now
   to each other.*

   *We endow our knowledge our secrets
   and all*

   And both of us together shall stand tall

   Free from mistrust deception and lies.

   By this spell, I strengthen our ties

   Together we stand now and forever

   Here to support one or the other!

6. Place everything in the green box and keep the box hidden (you can even place a protection spell on the box if you want), but be sure to put it out in the sun for a few minutes at least once a week.

PEACE AND UNDERSTANDING

This spell takes three days to complete, so you need patience with it.

For this spell, you will need the following:

- Two white candles
- Altar
- Water
- Salt
- Frankincense
- Resin
- A censer (a container that you burn incense in)
- Coals
- A pale blue candle
- Astral candle for each person that is involved
- A piece of lepidolite

Casting directions:

1. Cast your circle. Using the lit white candles, light the pale blue candle and the frankincense. Allow them to burn alone for a minute while you visualize a peaceful resolution to your current situation.

2. Visualize all the parties reconciling and peace returning. One at a time, you need to light the astral candles. With each candle you light, you need to say aloud whom they represent.

3. As you light each candle, visualize the person that it represents. Take a few minutes and meditate. Focus on bringing peace and calm into your area. Focus on peace overcoming every person that is involved in this conflict. Place some of the salt into the water while saying:

   May any impurities be cast out of this water that it may serve my purpose.

4. Hold the water in your hands and walk around the circle. Cast the water as you go around the circle and say these words:

   Purified water cast out the stress and strife that exists between myself and my family/friends.

   Cast out the arguments. Cast out the misunderstanding. Cast out the ill will.

5. Return to your altar and repeat the following chant:

   From out of the dark and into the light,

   A circle cast, a candle burns bright.

I look toward the sky, my song do I sing.

Spirits soar high, and gifts do I bring.

I offer my all! My mind, I then clear harken my call!

I feel you are near! The candle burns higher; my spirits set free!

Hotter than fire, this magic will be!

Let magic come round, from under the ground,

To form with my sound and then, to be bound!

Around me, I feel the magic so real,

Before you I kneel, the spell I now seal!

Let all hatred cease! And let there be peace!

Bring understanding and love, so below as above!

These words that I say with magic today!

This spell that I send is now at an end.

Let the magic I have laid go forth and not fade!

6. Once the incantation is over, sit down in front of the candle flames and visualize the results you hope to see from your spell. Repeat this spell again for the next two nights. On the second night, move the astral candles to cover half the distance to the pale blue candle, and on the third night, move it to cover the distance all the way. Allow the candles to burn out on the third night completely.

THINKING OF YOU

For this spell, you will need the following:

- A jar
- Honey
- Marker
- Popsicle stick
- Sugar

Casting directions:

1. Add the honey and sugar to the jar. On the side of the Popsicle stick, write out your full name.

2. Write the full name of the person that you want to think about you on the other side of the Popsicle stick.

3. Place the Popsicle stick inside the jar and seal it well.

4. Shake the jar and say the enchantment:

   Sweet, sweet thoughts of me,

   Oh, you will think them constantly.

NO TO NEGATIVE ENERGY

No relationship can survive if it is plagued by negative energy. This is true whether it is a friendship or a romantic relationship.

You might have been in a situation where you just wished that the negative vibes would disappear, and that is where this spell comes into play.

Wicca is based on a belief that what you put out into the world, you will also receive that back. In fact, it goes so far as to say you will receive it back times three. So if your thoughts and feelings are negative, then that is what you will attract. And it then becomes important to manage your negative energy and cast it out so that you can attract the good toward yourself.

For this spell, you will need the following:

- Sea salt

- Five white candles

Casting directions:

1. With the sea salt, draw a circle that is large enough for you to comfortably sit in while doing a meditative position. Sea salt is inherently supposed to be clean, so its purpose in this spell is to transfer energy. Your negative energy goes into the sea salt, and its positive vibes transfer into you. Remember how science says that energy can never be destroyed? Well, it is the same. You can only transfer negative energy, not destroy it.

2. Place the five white candles around the sea salt circle in as much of a pentagram shape as possible. These candles help you clear the air.

3. Sit in the center of the circle, and for fifteen minutes, meditate. Visualize the energy exchange between you and the sea salt. Feel your body relax and a calming sensation enveloping you.

4. Blow the candles out once you are done meditating. Please throw the sea salt out as it is now full of negative energy and cannot be reused.

WITH ALL MY LOVE

Sometimes people who are participants in a friendship or relationship have to be apart. This can be due to a myriad of reasons, but the basic necessity that these relationships need to thrive is love. You want to let your friends, family, or lover know that you love them. This spell will let them feel your love.

This spell is simple, yet it means a lot to those on the receiving end. You can use this spell to send your love to a friend who is feeling down, a sick family member, or a loved one that is far away. This can be a spouse you are apart from, a friend that lives across the country, or even a friend across town that you do not get to see very often!

For this spell, you will need the following:

1. One pink candle
2. A paper
3. A pen
4. A handful of rose petals
5. Rosemary
6. Bowl
7. Lighter

Casting directions:

1. After you cast the circle, center your mind and your energy. Focus only on good emotions and keep thoughts of love and peace. You need to focus on the person that you want to send your love to.

2. Write your person's name on a piece of paper. You can add drawings, runes, symbols, poetry, and reinforcing words (like *strong*, *happy*, and *carefree*) to the paper. While you are holding the paper in your hand, sprinkle the rose petals onto the center of the paper. Sprinkle the rosemary on top of the petals. As you do this, you need to chant:

   A rose is strong; a rose is love

   A symbol of the Goddess above.

   And this herb of a comforting feeling,

   Friendship, love, and healing

   Rose petals and Rosemary

   May it all be peaceful and merry.

3. The paper must get rolled thinly until it resembles a cigarette, and it is wrapped around the petals and rosemary. The paper needs to be kept together and not allowed to unwind open. Hold the paper over the bowl and use the lighter.

4. Burn one end of the paper and let it burn like incense. It needs to burn all the way to ashes. As the paper is burning, repeat this enchantment:

   And as the fire grows and grows

   May my love and will be shown

   By the goddess, I ask that [their name] gets what they need

   May love come and [their name] be free.

5. Once all the rose petals, paper, and rosemary are burned up, your message has been sent.

RECONCILIATION

For this spell, you will need the following:
- Altar
- Two pink candles

Casting directions:
1. This spell takes three days. On the first night, you need to light the two pink candles (pink is the color of Venus in her gentler aspect)—one for yourself and the other candle for the person that you want to reconcile or reconnect with.

2. Place the candles apart, at opposite ends of your altar. Speak toward the one that you designate for the absent person. Say the things you'd like to say if he or she were present. Do not hold back, speak them whether they are words of regrets or forgiveness or even both.

3. Then you need to speak into your own candle and recall all of the good qualities of the other person.

4. Blow out your own candle. This will send a message of love to that person, wherever he or she might be. Visualize them receiving this love.

5. Blow out his or her candle, and make sure you are absorbing positive feelings from all the good times you shared together.

6. On the second night, move the candles so that each candle has been placed toward the other a quarter of the way across the table, so they move closer together.

7. Light each candle again, but this time, speak toward the other person's candle and give thanks for the kindnesses they have shown to you in the past. Then into your own candle, say what you miss most about the relationship, as well as what you would like to rekindle with this person.

8. Blow out your candle, sending positive energy and wishes for the other person's happiness. Absorb the light from the other person's candle and visualize this as the healing of the unfair or harsh words that may have been spoken in anger. Blow out both candles.

9. On the third night, speak into their candle. Make your promises to try to be more tolerant and understanding in the future even if you think the disagreement or estrangement was not your fault. You want to focus on reconciliation and let go of any bitter feelings that you may hold.

10. This time, leave the candles so that they burn down. Sit in the candlelight and look at old photographs of the two of you. Or you can read poetry or listen to music that you both enjoyed.

11. When the candles have burned down, initiate a simple non-confrontational gesture of friendship. This can be sending a postcard of a place you both visited or an e-mailing them, recounting mutually pleasurable news about a family member or joint friend. You can even send a small trinket of affection toward them. You have freed yourself of bitterness if the gesture of reconciliation is refused. However, if the hurt is deep and you truly want them to reconcile with you, you may need to repeat the ritual several times.

MANIFESTATION POTION

For this spell, you will need the following:

- A bag of green tea
- One pinch of sage
- One pinch of cinnamon
- One pinch of thyme
- Three drops of your blood
- Three candles
- Crystals

Casting directions:

1. Open the bag of green tea, and if you need additional space if the tea bag is too full, you may take some of the tea leaves out of the bag. Add the sage, cinnamon, and thyme to the bag of green tea. You may also add ground-up rose petals or lavender if you want to give this potion an extra kick. Be careful and do not use cannabis or sugar; they will change the nature of the spell. Tie the bag back up and set it to the side for now.

2. Prick yourself gently and add three drops of your blood into a glass that is filled with warm water. Do not use a cut that is already open or a wound that has

scabbed over. If you add any infectious blood, then you taint the spell.

3. Transfer the water mixture into a microwave-safe cup and add water until the cup has enough to make one serving of tea. Microwave the water until it boils. Once it is steaming, add the tea bag to the water.

4. Let the tea steep for at least six minutes.

5. Stir the tea, and as you stir it, focus your positive energy into it. You do not want to create a spell borne out of selfishness or a dark place. As you stir, say this:

   By the power of the gods/goddesses,

   All bend their will to me.

   At first taste of this tea,

   Truth be clear, loyalty bound

   Sanity will not be found

   Their souls belong to me

   So might it be.

6. Place the three candles and a few crystals around the cup and let it steep even longer for a stronger effect. Do not worry if the potion has anything floating in it, like loose leaves. This is okay, and it will not detract from the potion's strength.

7. If you want, you can pour the potion into a bottle so you can transport or store it easily for later use.

8. This potion can work on anyone. You just need to add a few drops to their drink, or you could even sprinkle a little on their salad. As you have the person take your potion, keep in mind what you are seeking from them. Be very specific here. You may be seeking the truth about something, questioning unwavering loyalty, needing a favor, or maybe even seeking their help in familial issues. The reason you need to be specific and careful is that you could even bring them misfortune or sickness if you focus on the wrong things while they take the potion. Invoke your deity while planting the potion. The possibilities of what this potion can do are endless as it is a manifestation potion that manifests your desires.

9. This potion cannot be served as a tea and must be used sparingly, only a few drops at a time.

ROSEWATER

This spell can be used to attract new love or a new friend. Be careful not to think of a specific person, but rather invite new opportunities into your life with this spell.

For this spell, you will need the following:

- A bottle of rosewater
- White cord
- Four green candles
- One pink candle
- Charcoal
- A small burner to burn the charcoal
- Dozen fresh rose petals
- Four drops of rose essential oil
- One stick of cinnamon
- A gold pen
- A bowl that is filled with fresh spring water
- A bowl filled with earth (dirt)

Casting directions:
1. After you have bathed in warm water, mist yourself with the rosewater.

2. Now that you are relaxed and refreshed, cast your circle clockwise and light one green candle in each of the four major compass points of your circle. Invoke the winds while you face each direction in turn. Use these words as you invoke the winds:

   Hail to the east wind

   Hail to the south wind

   Hail to the west wind

   Hail to the north wind

   I call for love and make this offering to you.

   And it harms none, so be it.

3. Place the charcoal burner in the middle of your circle and lay the charcoal inside of it. Light the charcoal. Use the flame from the charcoal to light the pink candle, and place it alongside the charcoal burner.

4. Breathe deeply until you feel that your energy and emotions are properly concentrated and are positive ones. As you face east, place seven of the rose petals to one side and rub rose oil on to the rest of the petals.

5. Crush the cinnamon stick above the oiled rose petals. Lay these over the smoldering charcoal (the charcoals should not be ablaze with fire).

6. As you focus on the word *love*, use the gold pen to write *love* on each of the seven rose petals that you had put to one side earlier. Drop them into the bowl of fresh spring water.

7. Sit in the middle of the circle. Focus on the scents from the rose petals and the spices. Breathe in deeply and keep your energy focused on love. Give yourself to your emotions. Open your hands, open your heart, and repeat this enchantment seven times:

   Oh, Angel of Love, I call upon you to fill me with love that I may feel a joyous heart.

   I ask that I may share this love with another who will come to me of their own free will, and together, we will know the beauty of a loving union.

   I ask this for the highest good of all.

8. With these words spoken, say your thanks and blow out the candles. End the spell by taking the white cord and winding it up together around your arms. It must be wound loosely so that you can still move your arms and hands.

9. Take the container of rose-scented water in both hands and hold it up for a moment while transferring good energy to it. Then let it slowly drizzle into the bowl of earth.

NEW FRIENDS

For this spell, you will need the following:

- A white candle
- A pendant or a ring on a chain
- Incense

Casting directions:

1. Invoke the gods or goddesses that you are aligned with before you start this spell. Light some appropriate incense for the spell that you will use to attract new friendship.

2. Use the incense to cast positive energy into the pendant or ring to make sure it has no other negative energy in it. Hold the candle, then send positive energy into it as well. Breathe in slowly. As you breathe out, send that surge of energy into the candle. Do this several times until you feel the candle radiating and pulsing with light and good energy.

3. When you are sure that there is nothing in your items beside good energy, you must chant:

    May the power I send into this candle
    bring good people my way and into my
    life let these positive people stay.

4. Put the candle down and light it. Pick up the pendant that you will use. It should be on a chain.

5. Hold the pendant tightly in your hand and meditate for a minute. Visualize new friends coming into your life and focus on what it will look like to meet them. Then hold the chain on one end. The pendant should hang from the chain and not in your hand.

6. Hold the pendant near the flame (not too close) and slowly circle the candle with the pendant three times and chant:

    One, two, three,

    Draw new friends close to me.

7. Circle the candle with the pendant three more times again and chant:

    Four, five, six

    New friends to me will now be fixed.

8. Circle the candle with the pendant this last three times and chant:

    Seven, eight, nine

    New friends to me now are mine.

9. Do this action nine times in total. When you are done, hold the pendant in your hand and focus on

drawing in more positive friends. You may focus and use this time to ask the gods to help you as well.

10. Place the jewelry on and wear it proudly. Leave the candle burning until it burns out. Go out, and see who might cross your path. You might meet some interesting new people. This spell works rather quickly.

ATTENTION

Have you ever been in a bind, but it seems like no one is around to help you out? This spell is not so that you can get a lover to focus on you, but rather to draw attention in times of crisis or when you really need it.

For this spell, you will need the following:

- An orange candle
- A magnet
- A piece of hematite jewelry or hematite

Casting directions:
1. Set your altar up as you see fit. Then invoke the gods that you are aligned with. Never invoke a divinity that is not from your faith or one that you know nothing about as this can cause issues.

2. Give your gods your offerings and prayers.

3. Light the orange candle, and focus on the flame. Stare into it for at least two minutes. Watch the flame dance. Hold your hands on the sides of the candle and chant three times:

> *I am the sun; I am the key.*
>
> *All attention be focused on me.*
>
> *See what I do, and hear what I say.*
>
> *Let all heads turn and face my way.*
>
> *I am the center; I am light.*
>
> *I am this flame, dancing so bright.*
>
> *I sparkle interest, wherever I go*
>
> *Let all look at me, be it sunny or snow.*

4. As you focus on the orange candle, send energy that draws others to you into the candle. You can do this by visualizing people coming to you. Do this for as long as you can manage to keep up your visualization.

5. Put the magnet in front of the candle and cover it with your hand. Send into the magnet the power of attraction. Chant three times:

> *Magnetism is currently all mine*
>
> *Drawing the attention I deserve.*
>
> *And those that give me such*
>
> *Will be the first that I serve.*

> *People's attention now drawn to me*
>
> *And as my will, so might it be.*

6. Place the hematite over the top of the magnet and chant three times:

   > *Stone of iron, ore from the ground*
   >
   > *To draw attention make this spell sound.*
   >
   > *As you go with me all day, all night*
   >
   > *In work and business, give me your might.*
   >
   > *You shall make all pay attention to me*
   >
   > *To hear my words and record my deeds*
   >
   > *And give me the credit that I'm due*
   >
   > *To these tasks, I now ask of you.*

7. Do not move the magnet or hematite. Leave them in front of the candle until it burns itself out. Once the flame is out, take the hematite and carry it in your pocket. You could also alternatively place it in a sachet and carry that with you. Carry the stone with you and into areas where you are looking for attention.

8. You must not abuse this spell. If you do abuse it, it will not work. The stone may also end up disappearing on you.

CHAPTER THREE:
HEALTH AND WELLNESS

Health is important to us. After all, if we do not have health, then there are a lot of opportunities that limit us. In Wicca, there are a certain number of spells and enchantments that can help you with your mental and physical wellness.

We all want to stay in the best shape that we can. As a Wiccan, your energy sensors are heightened, so when negative energy infests you, you tend to be more affected by it than usual. So it is very important to know how to rid yourself of these negative emotions and energies.

SPELLS FOR WELLNESS

SLEEP WELL

For this spell, you will need the following:

- Lavender
- Chamomile tea

Casting directions:

1. This spell can vary, depending on the form of lavender that you have. Lavender that is in a liquid form should be dabbed lightly across your pillow. The lavender flower needs to be set inside your pillowcase where your head rests.

2. You need to boil some water to make your chamomile tea. It is crucial that you do not use sugar. This will taint the spell.

3. You need to sit on your bed and cross your legs as if you were about to meditate. Breathe in and breathe out. Focus on life flowing into you as you breathe in, and focus on your muscles relaxing as you breathe out.

4. If stress is plaguing you, visualize the stress as black smoke that you blow out. Then focus on breathing in positive and healing smoke. As you breathe in the positive smoke, visualize your stress fading and your body glowing with health.

5. Imagine that you are sitting in a calm wooded area. There are large trees, dappled sunlight filtering in, and the faint song of birds lulling you to sleep. Keep visualizing this scene as you calm yourself. Do this until the water for your tea has boiled.

6. As you wait for the tea to cool down enough to drink, breathe in the smells of the chamomile. Take long, deep breaths of the chamomile. This will have a calming effect on you. Slowly and quietly drink your tea. Do not overwhelm your mind with other thoughts.

7. Once your tea is finished, lie down on your bed. Focus on each muscle in your body. Feel for the moment when each muscle relaxes. Concentrate on letting go of stressful positions your body might want to revert back to.

8. Try to be at peace with yourself. As your head lies on your pillow, focus on the smells of lavender, and transport yourself through meditation to a place that is calming to you.

CASTING OUT FEELINGS

For this spell, you will need the following:

- Crystal
- Paper
- Black candle wax

Casting directions:

1. Write down everything that upsets you on the paper. This can be grievances with another person, stress, and even feelings that keep you up at night.

2. Hold the crystal in your hands and focus on it. Transfer all your negative energy into the crystal. Visualize the energy leaving your body and taking residence in the crystal. You can then seal the energy in the crystal by dripping the black wax all over the crystal to seal it. It takes a second because you want the wax to envelop the crystal like a ball.

3. Once your crystal resembles a ball of wax, you can freeze it. Over the next month, whenever you feel tense or upset, take the crystal wax ball from the freezer and transfer your energy into it. The crystal will keep hold of all your energy you give it.

4. Bury the crystal after thirty days in a place where it will not be disturbed. You can make a new crystal wax ball every month if you need to.

CLEANSING BATH

For this spell, you will need the following:

- A pinch of basil
- A pinch of thyme
- Pinch of garlic powder
- A handful of Epsom salt
- Ground dandelion root
- Essential oils of your choosing

Casting directions:

1. Run a bath with water that is as hot as you can stand it. As the bottom of the bath fills up, sprinkle in your basil, thyme, garlic powder, and the Epsom salt. Mix together the herbs in the bathtub, and take deep breaths of the aromas they let out. Add in your chosen essential oils to the herbed water and then sprinkle the ground dandelion root in the middle of the water.

2. Close your eyes and sink into the tub of water. Relax as you submerge your entire body but leave just your head out. Concentrate on the smells around you as you take deep calming breaths. Channel the spiritual energy that is within you. Feel the energy flowing

through your body. Begin by focusing on your toes and move up until your entire body is buzzing with energy.

3. At this point, you should have worked up a sweat on your brow. Visualize this sweat as negative energy that is leaving your body. Continue to breathe in and out deeply, visualizing your negative energy, leaving you with every breath you take.

4. Feel free to do this for as long as you need to. There is no set time limit for how long you can meditate and visualize. Before you exit the bathtub, speak these words:

   This water has washed all my negative energy away.

DIVINE HEALING

This spell is a little more advanced, but if you have been practicing your magic as you should, then you should be able to get it with a little bit of effort. This spell is great to heal both physical and mental wounds. You can use it on yourself or on another person, but you do need to be cautious with it because it is a very strong spell.

This spell only works if it is done during a full moon. It is known to help aid and cure several ailments, such as headaches and migraines, lower back pain, pain after surgery, psoriasis, inflammation, bowel issues, and much more.

For this spell, you will need the following:

- Five white candles
- One praying amulet
- One clear crystal ball
- One quartz point
- Hot water
- Ginger
- Turmeric
- Basil
- Birch leaf
- Wintergreen essential oil
- White willow bark
- Capsaicin
- Gamma-linolenic acid
- Cherry
- Arnica
- Peppermint

- Boswellia
- Bromelain
- Cranberry juice
- Mortar
- Pestle

Casting directions:

1. Cast your circle, and place your candles around the circle. Each candle should be placed in a zone for the elements. The candles must be lit in a specific sequence—spirit, earth, air, fire, and water. Wear the praying amulet that you have during this spell. At this point, you should have the crystal ball out and ready and your quartz in your hand. Close your eyes and visualize the light emanating from the ball. Say this enchantment while you touch the crystal ball with your free hand:

    By the power of Holy Light,

    And the power of the Holy Goddess,

    Please cure this injured human,

    Do not let them suffer for their whole life.

    Please cure them, cure them with all your power,

Fight the fear. Let the light flow,

Killing darkness in its path,

Let the dark fade away,

As I will it, so might it be!

2. Using your mortar and pestle, grind the ginger and turmeric together. Add the basil, willow bark, capsaicin, gamma-linolenic acid, birch leaf, essential oil, cherry, arnica, peppermint, Boswellia, bromelain, and cranberry juice to the mortar and pestle as well. Grind all these ingredients together well.

3. Pour this water into a crystal glass, and then drink the mixture. Or have the ailing person drink the mixture. Be careful with the amount of willow bark that you put in the mixture. Only use a quarter teaspoon of the bark.

CLEANSING MEDITATION

Sometimes stress gets the better of us. There are common techniques that the world uses to try to lessen the stress we feel. For example, you might try a very hot shower. But what happens when those methods do not work, and you still feel bogged down by stress?

For this spell, you will need the following:

- Jasmin incense
- Wormwood (you will burn this like it is incense)
- Incense burner
- Labradorite
- Quiet space

Casting directions:

1. Set aside a clear space for you to practice your meditation. Start burning the jasmine incense once you have a quiet spot set up.

2. While burning wormwood, make sure that you have your windows open. Wormwood does act as a hallucinogen, so if your space has no windows, reduce the amount of wormwood that you burn. When you burn wormwood and jasmine together, they work as one to dispel negative auras and energy that might lurk in the shadows.

3. Once the incense is burning, visualize what you want to get out of this meditation session. Relax your body and your muscles as you take up the position. The labradorite can be used for a grounding stone if you need it. If meditation music helps you, such as isochrone tones, then by all means, make use of the music. Make sure that you are still able to focus on your breathing with the music playing. Make your breathing your only focus. Inhale the good energy and exhale the negative stress. With each breath, just focus more on your goals and discard the stress that weighs on your shoulders. If you place yourself in a deep meditative state, you might even fall asleep.

NIGHTMARES, BE GONE

For this spell, you will need the following:

- One small white candle
- One white or silver ribbon
- An object made from silver

Casting directions:

1. Turn the lights in your bedroom off and sit in the dark. Tie the ribbon around the candle and light it. Once lit, place the candle in a position to where you can look at it directly. Keep your gaze on the burning

flame. Your body should naturally relax as you focus on the flame.

2. Your eyes should now close, and you should focus on memories or dreams that evoke feelings of happiness and peace. Meditate this way for as long as you need to in order to feel completely relaxed.

3. Once you are relaxed and your mind's mental focus has improved, take the candle and walk toward a window. Make sure that you can see the moon from this window. Stare into the moon's light and chant:

> *The moon is my friend who listens to me and brings beauty into my dreams.*
>
> *The stars are here forever to shine, bringing serenity and peace of mind.*
>
> *When I close my eyes, they will not be gone, keeping me safe until the dawn.*

4. Repeat the chant as many times as you personally need to. This is a very individual spell. If the candle's flame has not yet burned out, extinguish it with your fingers. Remove the ribbon from the candle and tie it around your wrist. You need to sleep with the ribbon on.

5. The candle must remain on your windowsill until the next morning; only then can you clear away the

candle. In the morning, you should also remove the ribbon from your wrist. This ritual can be repeated several times a week, but make sure that you always use a new candle and a new ribbon.

6. Collect and save each ribbon from every night you do this ritual. Once you feel like your nightmares have left you for good, you need to gather the ribbons and bury them. This will keep them away from you.

SPELLS FOR HEALTH

As mental wellness is important, so is our overall emotional health! These spells and rituals can help us get over ailments that we do not see an end too.

DEPRESSION AWAY

For this spell, you will need the following:
- Protection incense
- Yellow taper candle

Casting directions:
1. This ritual works best when the area it is completed in is left alone for three days. If there is a reason that you have to clear the spell area, then you must leave the

yellow candle out at least. If you do not, then the spell will not work.

2. As you set up your work area for the ritual, you need to focus on positive thoughts. Do not let negative emotions creep into your space now as this can set a bad tone for the ritual.

3. Take a cleansing bath where you can meditate and ensure that you are filled with positive energy. Focus on the purpose of the spell while you bathe. Think about the outcomes you will experience. Take your time; this is all about you. Once your bath is over, you must go back to the area that you set aside to work from.

4. Cast your circle, and then light the incense. Visualize a yellow light that is surrounding your work area. Hold onto the yellow candle and focus on it. Transfer all your positive energy into the candle while you hold it. When you are done, you should place the taper candle in a candleholder to keep it steady.

5. Do not light the candle just yet; first, you need to repeat this enchantment:

   This candle represents the love and energy I have for myself.

6. As you light the candle, you must also say aloud:

   As I light this candle, the veil of darkness that is ever present in my mind is lifting.

   The darkness ceases to exist as the light of this flame glows.

   Long has the darkness filled my mind; my desire to be happy is intense like the heat of fire.

   As this candle burns, my spirits are lifting, and the negative energy is washing away.

   I will be happy; my life will be peaceful.

   I can see myself as I wish to be, that is happy and free!

7. Relax and watch the candle burn. Sit down in a meditative position as you do this. Visualize the shroud of darkness lifting from you; let the feelings of happiness pierce through the dark. When the candle has burned a third of the way, chant:

   As the flame of the candle is extinguished,

   The light burns forever in my mind.

Now you need to extinguish the flame with your fingers.

8. This ritual must be repeated for two more nights. On the last night of the ritual, once the candle has burned away and the leftover wax has cooled down completely, throw the leftover wax away into the trash. As you do this, visualize your depression being thrown away with the wax. You will overcome your depression if you remain consistent!

HEALING POTION

For this spell, you will need the following:

- A pinch of arrowroot dust
- 150 grams of basil water
- Small apple slice
- One berry
- 20 grams of almond water
- A bowl
- A knife
- A spoon

Casting directions:

1. In a small bowl, mix the almond water and the basil water together.

2. Place the apple slice and the berry into this water mixture and leave it in a cool place for about ten minutes. Take the apple slice and the berry out of the water, but let all its drops drip back into the water bowl.

3. Sprinkle in the arrowroot dust and stir until either clear or well mixed. Be careful with how much dust you put in. You do not want this to become a paste.

4. Place the mixture into a vial, and keep it in a dark and cool place until it needs to be used. When you use it, a small amount will be enough to heal headaches and any muscle or bone pain. If you accidentally created a paste, do not worry. You can still use it. Just rub the paste onto aches and pains, and it should still help heal the affected areas.

STRESS-FREE

For this spell, you will need the following:

- One red candle
- One white candle
- Lavender oil
- Cinnamon oil
- A piece of red jasper
- A piece of clear quartz

Casting directions:

1. The red candle needs to be anointed with the cinnamon oil and then placed directly in front of you. Light the candle and think about all the things that currently stress you out or cause you pain. As you hold the red jasper in your hand, focus on it and visualize all the stress leaving you and entering the red jasper.

2. Move the red candle farther away from you now and place the red jasper in front of the lit candle. Now, bring the white candle toward you, and rub it with the lavender oil. Once the candle is anointed with the lavender oil, light the candle. Visualize peaceful thoughts as you let your mind slip into a state of being stress-free.

3. Allow both of the candles to burn all the way down. Carry the clear quartz with you as a reminder that the stress has gone away from you.

HEALING

For this spell, you will need the following:
- A blue candle
- A white cloth
- A few bay leaves
- A marker
- A cup of tea with one teaspoon of honey
- A bowl
- Sage or sandalwood incense

Casting directions:

1. You need to start by burning the incense. As the incense burns, use this to cleanse the blue candle. The person that is ill should lie down. If you are doing this spell for you, make sure that you are sitting down. Use the white cloth to wipe away all negative energy from the candle. Make sure that as you wipe, you only wipe the candle in one direction.

2. Using the marker, write down all the symptoms from the inflicted person onto a bay leaf. Place this leaf in the center of your palm and repeat these words:

   In this bay leaf, I here bind,

   All of your sickness at this time.

3. Visualize the illness pouring into the leaf, and then place the leaf into the glass bowl. You should repeat this step until you feel satisfied that the illness has reached all the marked leaves.

4. Give the ill person a new bay leaf to write down the way that they wish they would feel. Make sure the inflicted person holds the bay leaf for some time to charge it with their personal positive energy.

5. Have the ill person drink the cup of tea and honey. As they drink it, say:

   With this draught, all illness leave.

   As I will, so might it be!

6. Burn the bay leaves in the bowl that are tainted will illness as they finish drinking the tea. Once the leaves become ash go outside, release the ashes into the air. When all the ashes are released, go back inside. The sick person needs to rest for a while now. Sleep is their best friend during this time.

7. Place the bay leaf that they wrote their wishes on underneath their pillow. It should be quite soon when they start to feel better.

FERTILITY

Fertility can be a sensitive issue, but for those who want to conceive but are struggling, this ritual is a good place to start.

For this spell, you will need the following:
- Fresh rose petals
- Water
- Carnelian
- Image of a fertility lady
- Egg
- Green paint or marker
- Evergreen tree
- Rose oil or rose fragrance
- Green candle
- A wreath of flowers

Casting directions:
1. Grind the fresh rose petals with a mortar and pestle. Brew the ground petals in water alongside the carnelian to create a well-concentrated potion.

2. Place this water outside so that it absorbs energy from its natural surroundings. You can do this spell for either yourself or another person; it will work the same way. On your altar, place a fertility image, like Venus of Willendorf. Have the water that was left outside ready, the rose oil in a burner, a green candle that is positively charged, and your egg, along with what you will need to mark them.

3. If this spell is for another, they should lie down in an area near your altar. Begin by placing the wreath of flowers on your patient. If this is for yourself, place the flowers on your own person. Ask that she visualize herself holding a child within the wilderness. Dress the green candle with the rose oil that should now be warm. Once the candle is anointed, you should carve the symbol of fertility into it. Also, paint the same fertility symbol over the eggshell. Make sure the paint you use is green.

4. Trace the symbol over the belly of the person who wishes to get pregnant. Massage the rosewater over the belly. If the partner she wishes to conceive with is present, then they should do this part of the ritual.

5. Crack the painted egg over her belly. Light the candle and place your hands on top of the belly as you say this incantation loudly:

Great Mother, Grail of Life,

We ask that you bless this woman with the gift of fertility.

Cradle of Souls, Nurturing One,

Teach her your ways and manifest the fruit of her womb.

Be the fresh spring rain, encouraging her soil to birth new life.

Be the light of the moon, growing womb to full light.

Be the sea that life came from, making her the source for generations to come.

In the name of the Great Mother of the Living,

She who Eve was made in the image of,

Blessed be!

The woman who wants to conceive should now say this prayer:

You know my deep desire for a child

A little one to love and to hold, to care for, to cherish.

Grant that my body may conceive and give birth

> *To a beautiful, healthy baby in your holy image.*
>
> *Guide me in all my choices so that this conception,*
>
> *my pregnancy, and my baby's birth are in line with nature's will.*
>
> *Heavenly Earth and Holy Mother,*
>
> *Hear this prayer of my heart, mind, and spirit. Blessed be.*

6. You need to complete this next incantation while putting positivity into the belly:

   > *Beloved Gabriel, announce the birth of this woman's child.*
   >
   > *Allow her to already hear its cries for her from heaven.*

7. The egg that was cracked now needs to be scooped up from the belly and buried beneath a tree that is evergreen. The potion that was created with the ground rose petals needs to be massaged into the belly for a whole month. If the woman has a partner with her, they should do this massage together every day.

CHAPTER FOUR:
PROTECTION SPELLS

SPELLS FOR PROTECTION

ANTI-ANXIETY

For this spell, you will need the following:
- A bottle that can be made into a pendant of a necklace
- One to three pieces of lapis lazuli (should not be chips)
- Paper
- Red ink
- Blessed water
- One blue candle

Casting directions:

1. Light the blue candle and take the lapis lazuli and place it into the bottle. Write the following words in red ink on some paper:

    Stop my shaking,

    Stop the fear.

    Stop the anxiety and make it clear.

2. Sign your name or personal sigil at the end and then draw two matching pentacles beside your signature. Let this dry, and then fold it so that the paper can fit in the bottle.

3. Fill the bottle with blessed water, and seal the bottle with a cork. Let the candle burn and generate a fair amount of wax, then dip the top of the bottle in the wax. Allow the wax to cool completely to seal the bottle. Hold the bottle up and chant:

    Stop the shaking,

    Stop the fear.

    Stop the anxiety and make it clear.

4. You can put the bottle on a chain and wear it if you wish.

PROTECTED DREAMS

For this spell, you will need the following:

- One tablespoon lemon juice
- One tablespoon sea salt
- One tablespoon vegetable oil
- One lightweight cauldron (or a glass bowl if you do not have cauldron)
- One piece of paper
- Black pen
- One black candle
- One red candle

Casting directions:

1. In your bowl or cauldron, mix together the lemon juice, sea salt, and oil. Then place this mixture on the floor in front of you. Find a position to sit in comfortably and place the candles next to the mixture—a red candle on the right side and the black candle on the left side. Rip the paper in half then set it to the side. Light both candles, starting with the left one.

2. Close your eyes and visualize two spheres glowing beside you. These are the candle flames. Watch as the candles spin around you, going a little bit faster each time they pass you in a circle. Then see yourself magically being released. On a piece of paper, write down or draw what you saw as you were released. On another piece of paper, write down what your biggest fear is.

3. Using the candles, light the paper on fire. For the scene where you were released, light it on fire using the red candle. For the paper that holds your fears, use the black candle. Then throw them into your cauldron or the bowl.

4. Take the cauldron or bowl outside and pour its contents into a hole in the ground. Cover the hole with dirt and let it be.

HEART PROTECTION

For this spell, you will need the following:
- Three black candles
- A small, sharp stone

Casting directions:

1. You need to use a stone that has sharp edges for this. The stone must be small enough to be easily carried on a person and not be detected at the same time. You can be versatile with this and use a sharp jewel or other precious stone that has sharp edges that can be hidden in jewelry. Any small rock that is jagged or sharp will work just fine for this spell as long as it can be easily carried.

2. During a night of a full moon, you should wait until midnight to light the three candles. Place the stone in the center of these lit candles.

3. Once the candles and the stone are in place, chant the following incantation aloud:

    Stone of the earth,

    Guard my heart with your strength,

    Protect it from evil and harm

    That no danger may pass,

    No threat may draw near.

4. Extinguish the candles and break them all in half. Wear or carry the stone any time you feel the need for added strength and security against someone you know will make your heart weak.

PROTECT A ROOM

For this spell, you will need the following:

- Four pennies
- Five candles to represent each of the elements
- A small amount of powdered lemon rind

Casting directions:

1. Put a penny in each corner of the room. If your room is not shaped like a square, place a penny at either side to each entrance of the room. Remember to place pennies next to the windows as well. If you need to, you can use more than four pennies.

2. Cast a circle using the five candles as you normally would. As you summon the elements, ensure that you are respectful and you list one way in which each element will help you with your protection. Air should be the first element to enter the circle and the last to leave it.

3. Speak aloud that you need help protecting this room. Sprinkle the lemon rind around the circle that you cast in order to gain clarity on who your enemies are and whom you need to protect the room against.

4. Dismiss the elements in the same way you summoned them, respectfully, and be thankful to each element. The room should now be cleansed of all negative energy, and it can now be used as a protective barrier for whoever most often occupies the room.

CURSE BREAKER

For this spell, you will need the following:
- Cleansing incense
- Black candle that represents negativity
- White candle to represent positivity
- A sachet that is made up of the following:
    - St. John's Wort
    - Lavender
    - Rose
    - Bay
    - Verbena
    - Lemon
    - Bowl of water
    - Bowl of salt
    - Knife
    - Glass or china plate

Casting directions:

1. Light your incense and your candles. Place the black candle on the left side of your altar and the white candle on the right side.

2. Pass the sachet through the incense smoke to cleanse it and put it to the side to be used later.

3. Hold the lemon in both of your hands and allow the lemon to envelop the negativity. Visualize all the negative things that have happened to or around you and move them into the lemon, particularly if you suspect they are associated with the curse. To be on the safe side, just make sure all your negative emotions are put into the lemon.

4. Place the lemon on the plate.

5. Dip your knife into the water, then use it to slice the lemon into three separate pieces.

6. Touch each piece of lemon with the tip of the knife. As you touch each lemon, say this chant:

   Three times three, now set me free.

7. Visualize the negative energy drawing away from you and into the cut lemon. Repeat this chant as you push the negative energy out:

> *As sour as this lemon be,*
>
> *Charged and cut in pieces three,*
>
> *With salt and water, I am free.*
>
> *Uncross me now, I will it be.*
>
> *Lemon sour, lemon sour*
>
> *Charged now with power*
>
> *Let this lemon do its task*
>
> *Its cleansing power I do ask*
>
> *As this lemon dries in air.*
>
> *Free me from my dark despair.*
>
> *Uncross! Uncross! I break this curse*
>
> *But let not my simple spell reverse.*
>
> *I wish no ill, nor wish them pain*
>
> *I wish only to be free again.*

8. Take each lemon slice and dip it into the salt. You need to make sure that each slice is coated thoroughly in the salt. Set the slices back onto the altar and say:

   > *As it is my will, so might it be.*

9. Leave the lemon pieces on the altar until they can dry. Once the lemons are all dry the spell is complete, and the lemon should be thrown away or buried in the ground.

10. If, however, the lemon has rotted, you must repeat the ritual because this means that you are still cursed. While you are waiting for the fruit to dry, keep the sachet with you at all times to ensure that there is cleansing energy near you. It will protect you from the effects of the curse and turn away any negativity sent in your direction.

SALT PROTECTION

For this spell, you will need the following:

- Salt

Casting directions:

1. Sprinkle salt around yourself or others and try to make the circle complete. It must have no gaps within it while you say the following incantation:

    In the time, on this hour

    I fill this salt with ancient power,

    With this salt, a circle is made,

    To protect all within both night and day.

    No evil shall pass, no spirit shall see

    All who's in this circle. So might it be.

REVERSE A HEX

For this spell, you will need the following:

- Purple candle
- Rosemary oil
- White paper
- Black ink
- A fire-proof dish, such as your cauldron or even an ashtray

Casting directions:

1. Visualize all the blocks in your path being removed. Anoint your candle with the rosemary oil. On the piece of paper, write in black ink:

   All blocks are now removed.

2. Fold the paper three times away from you, and then light the candle and burn the paper in your dish. As you burn the paper, invoke the power of fire and its elemental spirits by repeating three times:

   Firedrakes and salamanders,

   Aid me in my quest,

   Protect me from all evil thoughts.

   Turn away and send back this hex.

3. After the third repetition, close your eyes and visualize the hex leaving your soul. No one has the right to curse another person. All you are doing with this spell is turning the negativity back where it belongs. Remember that whatever is put out will be returned in three.

DOOR PROTECTION

For this spell, you will need the following:
- Three white tealight candles
- Red sand
- Salt
- Bay leaf
- Coriander
- Garlic
- Lavender
- Incense (jasmine)

Casting directions:
1. First, crush and mix all the herbs in a bowl. Add the sand and the salt. While you are mixing these ingredients, focus on the area that you want to protect and visualize it being safe.

2. Light the incense and place it to the left-hand side of the door. Create a line of the sand and herbs across the threshold of the door. You can lay the sand and salt by the door frame under the carpet or mat that is by the door.

3. After this, lay the three candles across the doorway. Pick up the incense to draw and visualize a protective symbol of your choice across the door. While you do so, chant:

> *Bless this home property of mine.*
>
> *Protect and guard this doorway.*
>
> *By the powers of three,*
>
> *Powers of three,*
>
> *Powers of three,*
>
> *May I wield a shield of steel and strength*
>
> *To shield me from those of cruel intent.*
>
> *Banish those who mean me harm*
>
> *If not invited you shall not pass.*

4. Leave the candles by the door so that they burn all the way. Make sure that the tealights are not in danger of burning the carpet or anything else in their vicinity.

PROTECT A FRIEND

For this spell, you will need the following:

- Ten white candles

- A pink or red candle

- A connection to the elements

Casting directions:

1. You need to start by being outside at night and chanting these words to the moon:

    Spirit of the moon, lend me some of your power until the end

    So that I can, with the power of my love, protect a friend,

    [Friend's name] is her name in my heart forever.

    I place this shield of magic on her so that she will never

    Get hurt by any harm from this world or another,

    Spirits of the earth, you are life and all the plants' mother.

Spirits of the water, you are healing and the cleansing power,

Spirits of the wind, you are the rulers of the sky and can go higher than any tower.

Spirits of fire, you are death and destruction, but you are also light.

I am asking you elements to come to my aid; help my friend in her fight.

I ask for your powers to guard and help my friend in any time of need and make all evil go away,

And guide her as she makes her way throughout the day.

I place this shield upon her as a protection from my heart

So that there will always be from me apart, with the power of the three,

So might it be.

2. Once you are done, place the candles on the ground around you and sit in the center. You need to then light the pink or red candle that you chose. Once you light this candle, light all the other candles.

3. Clear your mind and visualize the energy you feel from the moon. Connect with the nature around you and feed positive energy into the space you occupy. Say the above chant again. As you repeat the chant, envision a shield you create that you pass down to your friend in protection.

4. Thank all the spirits for their help as you finish your chant. Blow out each candle, remembering to blow the red candle out last.

5. Whenever you see your friend, visualize the shield protecting her so that you can ensure the protection spell stays strong.

CHAPTER FIVE:
MOTIVATION SPELLS

SPELLS TO MOTIVATE YOU

EXPAND YOUR THINKING

For this spell, you will need the following:

- Incense that calms you

Casting directions:

1. Begin this ritual to expand your mindset by lighting the incense that calms you the most.

2. Move into the position that you find most comfortable for meditation. Focus on yourself and your inner mind. This is opposite to most other meditations involving magic, so it might take you a second to find your focus.

3. Focus on your inner self as deep as you can. As you delve deeper in introspection, you will find a small part of you. It might take shape into whatever your inner psyche wants to appear as. Focus all your positive energy onto this piece that you find.

4. As you concentrate, split this piece into two smaller pieces. Keep focusing on the energy. Build each piece into bigger pieces and allow the smallest piece to be absorbed by the bigger piece.

5. You need to keep meditating to delve deeper and expand your ways of thinking. Be careful as you focus this intensely on yourself. Visualize the connection between the piece you have found and yourself. If you find that you see a different personality emerging, you need to sever this connection as you do not want to create a split personality.

6. The more you develop this mental peace within you and foster the connection, the easier it will be for you to store and recall information that you gain in your everyday life.

DECISION-MAKING

This spell takes three days to complete, so bear with it and stick it out. It will help you with your decision-making.

For this spell, you will need the following:

- Two yellow candles
- One white candle
- Length of purple ribbon
- Two pieces of paper
- Pen

Casting directions:

1. Lay the white candles on the middle part of the ribbon. The ribbon represents the highest possible spiritual energy you can touch. Place the two yellow candles on opposite ends of the ribbon. On the piece of paper, write down the two possible outcomes for the decision you need to make.

2. Place these two pieces of paper underneath the yellow candles. Light the white candle first, and then light the two outer (yellow) candles. Burn the candles for at least an hour so that a connection is properly linked. Visualize both decisions carefully.

3. Snuff the candles out with your fingers and move the papers and the yellow candles closer to the white candle on the second day. Roll the ribbon toward the center against the bases of the yellow candles. Relight the candles (starting with the white one again) and let them burn for at least an hour. Visualize all your options carefully.

4. Repeat this one more time on the third day, bringing all of the candles together. Ensure that the candles have enough left to burn for at least an hour on the final day. Allow the candles to burn out, and at the end of three days, you should find your decision a simple one to make. This spell provides the energy needed for the correct decision. It allows you to be rational and objective and allows you to find what your inner self is telling you to do. It keeps your mind focused on the decision you need to make. When you use this spell, you remove yourself from blocking your path to success.

MOTIVATION BOOSTER

For this spell, you will need the following:

- Incense
- Paper
- A match or a lighter
- Ink pen
- A tealight candle
- A cauldron or a pot

Casting directions:

1. Get all of your materials out on your altar and cleanse and consecrate the materials to remove any negative energies and establish your intent with them. If you need to, you can light your gods' and goddesses' candles, but they are not necessary.

2. First, light your incense and candle. Then write on a full-sized sheet of paper the tasks that you have left to accomplish.

3. Place your cauldron or pot directly in front of you. Hold the paper in one hand and the incense in the hand that is your power transfer. Focus on the tasks that you wrote and twirl the incense around the paper in a clockwise motion.

4. Fold the paper toward you three or four times. Light a corner of the paper on fire. Immediately release the paper into the cauldron. Once the fire is in the cauldron or pot, chant:

   Remove this feeling of tired and drained,

   I desire to feel refreshed as a summers rain.

   My request is to move quickly and with purpose

   From here on out, laziness will suppress.

   My fingers become nimble and quick

   As the fire burns from this candlestick.

   This spell harms none

   And motivates one

   As I will it, so shall it be!

5. Look into your cauldron and make sure all pieces of paper are burned. There can be no pieces of paper left. Ashes must be the only thing that remains. If any pieces of paper remain intact, burn them thoroughly. Repeat the chant once more while burning any remnant pieces of paper.

6. Repeat this spell for an entire week and save the ashes. Collect the ashes in your hand and blow the pieces into the wind from your window, or you can go outside.

EMOTIONAL IMPROVEMENT

For this spell, you will need the following:

- One red candle
- Hematite
- Pepper
- Paper

Casting directions:

1. Remember that all spells rely on your energy, so it is important to meditate before you start this spell as meditation created energy, and your energy will improve the success of this spell.

2. Cast your circle while you call the elements to aid you. You can invoke a deity you are aligned with that represents happiness and joy. If you have not chosen a deity, learn about Hathor and then invoke Hathor. Hold your candle tightly in your hands and transfer the energy from your meditation into the candle. Visualize the energy leaving you and entering into

your candle. Once the candle is charged, you will want to anoint the candle with the pepper.

3. You need to light your candle and, at the same time, visualize the happiness that you will feel with the spell. Write down on the paper what you want this spell to accomplish. Fold the paper toward you, and turn it clockwise. Fold it toward yourself one more time. Light the paper with the flame from the candle and chant:

> *Great goddess Hathor, I ask that you bring your presence to this room.*
>
> *Upon this night, help me with my magic.*
>
> *Fulfill my intention.*
>
> *Offerings I will leave to you.*
>
> *All I ask is your help.*
>
> *So might it be.*

4. Continue to chant:

> *Upon this blessed night with goddess Hathor's might,*
>
> *Great Goddess, hear my plea.*
>
> *Courage from you is what I seek.*

Expel emotion and negativity.

Fill me with confidence and happiness.

This is my plea, so might it be.

5. Leave an offering to Hathor after you have finished your incantation.

POSITIVITY

For this spell, you will need the following:

- A quiet place
- A happy memory

Casting directions:

1. As you sit down, close your eyes and remember a time where you felt genuine happiness or real peace.

2. Now imagine having the version of you that is from that memory simply walking up to you. You have a soft, warm ball of light in your hands. In the present, hold out your hands in a cupped shape, and visualize your memory self handing the light to you. As you hold it, you feel all of the warmth and energy from the warm light seep into your hands and circulate throughout your body. As you keep strong focus on the light that you are engulfing, say this chant:

Today may not have been my best

But it always could have been something worse

And I know that when I feel distressed

I simply must travel in reverse

I'll journey back to yesterday

Recharge with light of my past glee

And nothing can take this joy away

For the one, it came from is none other than me

Let my light be eternal and ever-giving,

This is my wish, so might it be!

INCREASE CONFIDENCE

Our self-esteem can be destroyed by people who love us, the media that controls our perceptions of ourselves, and even an enemy whose aim is to harm us. But there are ways that we can combat the negative energy that takes away our self-esteem.

For this spell, you will need the following:
- Four purple candles
- Rose essential oil

- lemon essential oil
- Rose quartz or amethyst crystal
- Mirror

Casting directions:

1. When we believe in ourselves, we radiate a unique energy that draws others toward us. The energy manifests itself as magnetism. You need to fill your bathtub and place purple candles around the tub so that the light illuminates your bath water.

2. Once your bath is full, place five drops of rose essential oil and five of the lemon, dropping them into the pools of light that the candles cast across the water.

3. Place the rose quartz into your water to strengthen your own self-love and approval.

4. As you lie down in the water, focus on each flame from the candle and make affirmations to yourself about your qualities. They can be as simple as "I exist, I am of worth, I have gifts, I value myself, I am complete, I treasure who I am, I am unique." Visualize the light that you are focusing on enter you with positive energy.

5. As you exit the tub, focus on this chant:

   Doubts and sorrow, flow from me,
   what I wish, I can be.

6. Really look at yourself in the mirror, and you will see how your inner radiance has created true beauty that cannot fade.

7. Do not snuff the candles out. Carry them into the space you will occupy, and throughout the night, focus on the candles and their positive messages toward yourself. Let them burn out on their own.

INSPIRED

This spell works well for those of creative minds as it gets its background from creativity. Ceridwen (whom we call on in this spell) is said to have brewed herbs together gift inspiration to her ugly son Agfaddu. Gwion was supposed to look after the potion but, after being splashed by the potion, absorbed its powers instead. Once he escaped Ceridwen's wrath, he turned to a seed of corn and was swallowed by her as she pretended to be a hen. The Welsh bard, known as Taliesin, was born nine months later.

For this spell, you will need the following:

- Cauldron
- Seeds (preferably wheat)
- White candle
- Rosebuds
- Cedarwood chips
- Sweet myrrh

Casting directions:

1. Blend your incense the night before you will use it. Your incense is made out of the rosebuds, cedar wood chips, and myrrh. Light your incense and the candle at the same time. Place the cauldron in front of you. Fill it halfway with the wheat seeds. Stir the cauldron clockwise three times and allow the seeds trickle through your fingers as you chant:

   This spell pays homage to Ceridwen, a Welsh Goddess, and nurturer of Taliesin, a Druidic Bard.

   She is invoked here and asked for the gift of inspiration.

   Ceridwen, Ceridwen, I seek your favor.

   Just as you searched for the boy Gwion,

So I search for the power of Awen,

Inspiration to be what I must, to discover the known,

And to flow with change. Grant, I pray, this power.

2. Since Awen is a threefold gift, you need to stir the cauldron two more times so that you can complete three stirrings. Once you have finished, empty the remains of the incense into the cauldron and bury the contents of the cauldron in the ground. The candle can be snuffed out but can no longer be used for anything else.

MORE CONFIDENCE

For this spell, you will need the following:

- One piece of rose quartz
- One piece of amethyst
- One piece of emerald
- Salt
- One brown candle

Casting directions:

1. As you sit in meditation pose, place your quartz, amethyst, and emerald around you in a triangle. The quarts should be at the upper point of the triangle while the amethyst makes the left point and the emerald is the right point of your triangle. Light the candle and hold it in your energy hand as you chant:

   Flame so bright, flame so right,

   Take away the meek,

   Give me the wisdom and beauty of the Greek goddesses.

   Let the salt I shower upon myself carry

   What I crave, and upon my wake, I be changed

   From the shy, cautious one I am

   To the confident one, I wish to be.

2. Sprinkle the salt around and over yourself and blow the candle out gently. Go to sleep, and in the morning, you will feel invincible!

MOTIVATION IN UNUSUAL SPACES

For this spell, you will need the following:

- Clover
- A book
- A picture of yourself
- A lighter
- A bowl
- A small bag
- Cutting tool

Casting directions:

1. Take the bowl and put the clover and your picture inside it. Use the lighter to burn the clover and the picture until there are only ashes left. Let the bowl cool down before you touch it. Take the ashes and put them inside the small bag. Open the book and cut the pages. You want to cut so that there is a little box inside the book that is big enough for the bag to fit.

2. Place the bag of ashes into the hole you have cut in the book. Place the book underneath your pillow. Keep it there when you sleep and do not move it until you feel more motivated than you were before.

INCREASE WILL POWER

For this spell, you will need the following:

- A candle

Casting directions:

1. On your altar, place the candle and then light it. Repeat four times in a chant:

   Oh will power come to me

   I need you in my darkest hour

   Will power come to me so might it be!

2. Then channel your energy into the tasks that you need to do. If you meditate before you complete this spell, then you will increase the effects of the spell.

CHAPTER SIX:
LUCKY SPELLS

SPELLS ABOUT LUCK

CHARM OF LUCK

For this spell, you will need the following:

- St John's Wort
- Chamomile
- A drawstring bag
- A string or chain (to attach to the bag)
- Sage incense
- Red cord

Casting directions:

1. St John's Wort is often used in the medicinal field as an anti-inflammatory and antidepressant, so it is helpful in keeping away negative energies. You can start by adding these dried leaves into your drawstring bag. Chamomile is a soothing plant, and it calms people enough for positive energy to filter through. These will be the next plant that you add into your drawstring bag.

2. Use sage incense to cleanse the bag and its contents. Focus on the positive energies and visualize the good luck that you want the bag to bring to you. Attach a red cord to the bag and use it as a necklace that you wear with you wherever you go.

CHANGE MY FATE

For this spell, you will need the following:
- A wishing candle
- A pentacle
- Four black candles that are smaller than the main candle

Casting directions:

1. Set up your altar by placing a black candle in each corner of it. In the center, place the pentacle; and over it, place the wishing candle. This spell needs to be done during the full moon when the sky is at its brightest.

2. Once the night of the full moon arrives, look into the sky to find the seven brightest stars. Hold up a black candle and chant:

   I wish I may, I wish I might, have the wish I wish this night

   For change of [what you hope to change] this night, I ask,

   And by the flame, I ask it last.

   Seven brightest stars in the sky, light the flame I hold high.

3. With this lit black candle, light your wishing candle and light the other three black candles with the same flame. Let the candles burn for around an hour before snuffing them out.

GO AWAY, MISFORTUNE

For this spell, you will need the following:

- Three small jars
- Nine cloves of garlic
- Nine thorns from a white rose

Casting directions:

1. Pierce the garlic cloves with the rose thorn. Forcefully chant while you pierce the garlic:

   Misfortune, begone from me.

2. In each jar, place three garlic cloves and three rose thorns. Each jar with garlic cloves must be buried within sight of a church. Say the same chant above each time you do this. Walk away, and do not look back at the garlic jars you have buried.

3. This spell works fairly quickly. Look for a common theme where your misfortunes are occurring, and name them out loud in your chant to improve its effectiveness.

GOOD LUCK

For this spell, you will need the following:
- Paper
- Writing utensil
- A stone or pebble that will become your lucky object
- A lucky symbol, such as a horseshoe or four-leaf clover

Casting directions:
1. With the pen, draw a pentagram on your paper. Make sure that the image covers most of the paper. Put the symbol of luck on the right side of your paper and the object that you want to make lucky on the left side. Chant this spell three times in a row:

    Good luck is what I want.

    Please look upon my prayer.

    I wish to have luck

    Wherever I go,

    Whenever I carry this stone.

    If I do not follow the rules that are meant to be,

You have the rights to revoke my good luck.

I wish with all my might

To have good luck.

So might it be!

2. Then carry the lucky symbol with you to ensure that good luck follows you wherever you go!

LUCKY BAG

For this spell, you will need the following:
- A small square of paper
- One herbal tea bag
- Two eucalyptus leaves
- A pen
- Three clovers
- One carnelian
- One small charm bag
- One chain

Casting directions:

1. In a hot cup of water, steep your tea bag. Once it is nicely steeped, take the tea bag and stain the piece of paper with the bag. Place this stained paper onto the eucalyptus leaves. The paper must be folded in half and left to dry.

2. Remove the leaves from the paper once it dries out. Write down on the paper that you want good luck.

3. Roll the piece of paper up and put it into your charm bag. Add the carnelian and clovers to the bag as well. Tie the bag shut, and now you have a lucky charm bag!

CHAPTER SEVEN: ALL ABOUT LIFE SPELLS

SPELLS FOR SUCCESS

CREATIVITY BOOSTER

For this spell, you will need the following:
- Blue fabric
- Yellow ink or paint
- A citrine
- Cinnamon or bergamot oil
- Diffuser or oil burner

Casting directions:
1. On the piece of fabric, write a word or draw an image that represents where you need to focus your creativity. Anoint the corners of the fabric with the cinnamon or bergamot oil.

2. Place the cloth in front of the diffuser that is on your altar. Place the citrine on top of the fabric.

3. Light the candle of your diffuser, and as the oil is burning, you should meditate for a few minutes about your project. As you finish meditation, you should chant:

   Open my mind; let my creativity flow,

   My heart and mind direct; my hands create.

   The ideas will start flowing to you as you meditate, and you will be ready to start creating.

4. Once the oil is finished burning, take the piece of fabric with the citrine and place it near you or near your place of work. Repeat the meditation every week on the same day that you started the spell to boost your creativity. For every new project that you start, you need to get a new piece of fabric and write a word or draw an image that symbolizes your project. Do not forget to anoint the fabric with the oil!

QUIT SMOKING

For this spell, you will need the following:
- Tobacco
- Cigarette butts
- Thin black cloth
- Black candle
- White candle
- Mouthwash

Casting directions:

1. In the black cloth, wrap the tobacco and cigarette butts up and close the cloth. Inscribe symbols of willpower in the candles.

2. Light the black candle, and as you do, inhale the foul odor of the packaged cloth. Focus your energy on hating the packaged cloth and its smell. Say this incantation three times as you focus on pouring your addictive energy into the candle:

    This that harms me, I let go.

3. Snuff out the black candle when you are ready or feel drained. Bury the rest of the black candle in the dirt with the black cloth and its contents. You need to go brush your teeth and use mouthwash.

4. Take three deep breaths as you light the white candle. Bring positive energy and focus on spreading positive vibes into the candle. Chant three times:

   I am breathing, I am clean, I am free.

5. Repeat this with the white candle every morning and every night until you no longer feel the urges to smoke or are grossed out by the thought of a cigarette.

BANISH BAD HABITS SUCCESSFULLY

For this spell, you will need the following:

- White candle for purity
- Black to banish
- Green for health

Casting directions:

1. This spell works best during the waning phase of the moon; however, it will work no matter the phase the moon is in. Focus on what you consider your bad habits to be. List them down if you need to.

2. Light your white candle. You need to focus on what you gain from banishing your bad habits. Stay by your altar as you complete this spell. Meditate on change; meditate on acceptance. You need to embrace the changes you will see as your bad habits will leave you.

3. Light the black candle, but keep the white candle lit as well. Focus on banishing the energy that perpetuates your bad habits into the black candle. Hold it with both hands. Focus on nothing but your breathing and the candle as you transfer the energy.

4. As you light your green candle, you are focusing on good health. You need to transfer good energy. Meditate, so you do not get tired of losing energy from the transfers.

5. Keep all the candles burning at the same time. Focus on what each candle represents to you and replicate the energy for each one. Accept the purity from the white candle and let the energy renew you. Give the black candle your bad energy that causes the bad habits, and then allow the green candle to renew the energy that correlates to your vitality.

DREAM JOB

For this spell, you will need the following:
- Thick green candle
- Incense of bergamot or bay leaf
- Oil, such as bergamot, rosemary, bay leaf

Casting directions:

1. The first step in this spell is to cast your circle. Consecrate the green candle in the incense and charge it with your intentions by visualizing your need for a job. Use a needle and carve your name into the green candle. Using the oil of your choice, anoint the candle. These oils are linked to successful employment.

2. Light your candle and relight the incense. Focus on the flame of the candle. While you focus, do not think about *if* you get the job. Visualize yourself with the job. You need to chant three times in a row:

    > *I call upon the universe to help me find a stable job as a [job that you want].*
    >
    > *I need it to pay well enough to pay my bills and other living expense with maybe a little left over for fun.*
    >
    > *Let me work in harmony and be treated fairly with all others employed there.*
    >
    > *May they accept me as I am, and may I accept them as they are.*
    >
    > *I humbly ask for this to come to fruition as soon as possible.*

3. At the end of the spell, snuff out the candle but allow the incense to finish burning.

MAKE OPPORTUNITY HAPPEN

This spell can be used for any kinds of opportunities that you are seeking. It is especially helpful for business and work opportunities.

For this spell, you will need the following:
- A bowl of sand (to represent the earth)
- Green cloth
- Needle and thread
- Pen
- Cinnamon or cedar incense
- Dried chamomile
- Mint and honeysuckle oil

Casting directions:
1. From the cloth, make a satchel. Concentrate on the opportunities you have and the ones that you want. Add the dried herbs into the satchel and add a few drops of the oils. Sew the satchel shut once you have added the herbs and oils.
2. Light the incense you chose and swirl it around the satchel. Chant:

    Goddess of opportunity,

Bring good fortune now to me.

Guide me by your gentle hand,

For I am as worthy as these grains of sand.

3. As you say the chant, touch the sand gently and allow the grains of sand to wash over your fingers and back into the bowl. Repeat the chant seven times, and each time, use the incense and the sand rituals to keep the spell going.

4. Place the satchel in a safe place where you can visit every day. This way, you can benefit from the spell. It needs to be renewed every full moon.

EMPOWER YOURSELF

For this spell, you will need the following:

- Cinnamon
- Bag

Casting directions:

1. On a plate, lay out a large amount of the cinnamon and keep in mind that there should be no other spices in with the cinnamon. In the cinnamon, draw a rune that signifies power. As you draw the rune, visualize

ways in which you are being empowered. Take a moment to think about things that take your power away and banish these negative energies into the rune.

2. Draw a circle around the rune once you have done your visualization. Take your bag and put all the enchanted cinnamon into the bag. Close the bag to make sure that the energy is trapped inside. The bag should be taken outside and left somewhere in nature. As soon as the spell is complete and the bag is in nature, you should feel the effects of the spell.

PROSPERITY AND LUCK SACHET

This sachet is best done under a waxing moon.

For this spell, you will need the following:

- Small green bag
- Green ribbon
- Thread and needle to sew the bag shut
- Rosemary
- Cinnamon
- Basil
- One bay leaf

- One dandelion
- One clover
- Parsley
- Rice
- Chamomile
- Three pieces of pine cone
- A silver coin

Casting directions:

1. At your altar, light your altar candles. Take your bag and add into it the herbs and flowers. Focus on your goals and good luck as you add the herbs into your bag. Sew the bag shut or tie it shut with the ribbon.

2. Once the bag is shut, say this chant:

    By sun in me, my prosperity shall increase.

    By new moon in the gods, success will my magic now release.

3. Sit in a position for meditation and meditate with the sachet, infusing it with your personal power and energy. You have to be positive and make sure that you are only emitting positive energy to your sachet. Visualize happiness, success, and wealth as you

meditate. Keep building positive thoughts and feelings. This will put the law of attraction in motion for you. As you meditate, the bag will begin to grow warm. When you feel this happen you must chant:

I compel these magical herbs of prosperity and power

To assist me with my spell work in this hour.

Pair your natural magic gently with mine

So that wealth and success may come to me at all times.

By the enchantment of herbs, this spell has been spun.

This is my will, so might it be, and harm none.

4. You need to have this sachet on your person for an entire month, but it is crucial that once this month is over, you return the herbs to nature, where they came from. This can be as simple as sprinkling the herbs out into the wilderness. Wash the bag once you have emptied it of the herbs and spices.

BE HAPPY

For this spell, you will need the following:

- One white candle (one per person)
- Rosemary
- A charm
- A stick of sage incense
- A crystal (preferably quartz or amethyst)

Casting directions:

1. As you light the candles on your altar, hum a tune that is light and positive. The crystal needs heat for this spell to work, so you need to hold the crystal above the candle's flames as you hum. Keep the crystal there until you feel the tips of your fingers warm from the crystal's own heat.

2. Once it is warm, you can take the crystal and hold it against the charm you chose to enchant with happiness. Continue to hum your happy tune as you work with the charm and the quartz. If the tune evokes a happy memory for you, all the better. Channel these into the crystal. You can now blow the candle flame out.

3. You will feel the positive energy transfer into the crystal. From the crystal, the energy will set in your charm. Set the crystal down, and place your charm on. This can be in the form of a bracelet, ring, earring, or even a necklace or brooch. When you are feeling down, need some extra cheer, or just a little more smile in your day, hum the same song that you hummed as you did the ritual. Place your hands on both your charm and your heart for it to work. You will instantly feel lighter.

STUDY SUCCESS

The oils in this spell can be easily substituted for others that are geared toward success. You can use honeysuckle, which is for passing tests; lilac, which improves memory; orchids, which help with focus; and even hibiscus, which is for wisdom.

For this spell, you will need the following:

- Yellow household candle
- Concentration oil
- Concentration incense

Casting directions:

1. You should take the candle and carve your name into its side. Anoint the candle with the oil of your choosing. First, your incense needs to be lit, and then you can light the candle. While standing in front of your altar, say:

    Oh, Spirits of Wisdom, to you I pray that throughout my studies, my mind will not stray.

    Keep it receptive, open, and clear for me. As it is my will, so it shall be.

    Repeat this at least five times as you hold your candle and focus on it.

2. The candle should remain burning until you feel like the spell has worked and your request has been granted. This needs to be repeated daily until the candle has burned out all the way.

3. Remember the incantation for this spell, and repeat it as you are studying or just before you write a test or exam. It will renew the spell's energy and help you with what you sought from the deities. It gives you an even bigger boost if you anoint your temples and wrists with the oils that you chose to anoint your candle with.

4. You can use several candles. Just make sure you anoint them all in the oil. You can also leave one of the candles burning as you study.

SPELLS TO MEMORY

FORGETTING BAD MEMORIES

Memories can stick to us like glue, and while the nicer memories are great to have, we do not always want to remember the traumatic events of our childhoods.

This spell also helps us unblock memories that we have repressed. We need to deal with these repressed memories with positive energy and allow them to move on from us so that we can live in acceptance and move on ourselves. This ritual can work for anyone, and it is interesting to try, especially for those who think that they have no bad memories repressed inside of them.

For this spell, you will need the following:

- Yellow candles
- Black paint
- A box of any shape, or size
- A solar incense

- Music of a childlike nature (this may be used to enhance the atmosphere)

Casting directions:

1. Get yourself a box with a lid and paint the inside of your box black. You can use a shoebox as long as the lid works to close properly. If you do not have paint, an alternative is to line the box with a surface that reflects like aluminum foil.

2. Decorate the outside of your box with drawings and photos that evoke powerful childhood memories—happy or sad ones. You just need to trigger events you might not have thought about for a while. Light your candles and incense at your altar and have your box open as you chant your intentions:

   It is my will to greet my past and accept it for what it is.

   I call the past to meet the present,

   that the future may be bright.

   I bring myself forth from the dark,

   and hold me to the light.

   Let not the past control my present,

   let not my future be dark as night.

I meet and greet me with open arms,

and move back into the light.

3. Close the box as you say this chant and focus your mind on it. Think about everything you can remember from your childhood and place it into the box. Any teasing, fights, and even insults should be focused toward the box. You will not have pierced through to your repressed memories yet, and that is okay. This takes time.

4. Open the box. Visualize what is inside. You might feel pain or grief as some memories are unlocked. Only you can see what your box of memories will show you. Try not to get absorbed in the box. Accept that the memories happened and focus your energy on dispelling the negative effects that these memories have harbored inside of you for so long. Whatever you want to do with the box is up to you. Some people like to destroy the box; others like to keep it closed and unleash it on the sunniest day to let the light banish the dark memories. Be careful not to keep the box and continue to dwell and torture yourself with memories of the past.

CONCENTRATION AID

For this spell, you will need the following:
- Rosemary
- Basil
- Caraway seeds
- Dried lemon rind
- A small bowl to mix the herbs
- A small cloth bag
- A silver cord

Casting directions:
1. As you combine all the herbs together, add a little more rosemary than the other herbs. Chant the following:

    Help me now as I seek your aid.

    Let me bring you honor in what I have to say.

    Grant me clarity and teach me not to sway.

    The task at hand is what I need to focus.

    As I will it, so might it be done.

2. Once you are done with the chant, add the herbs to the bag, tying it securely with the silver cord, then place the sachet somewhere close to your work area. This will help ensure that you focus on your tasks and also give energy of wisdom into the area that you can draw on.

SPELLS TO FIND THE TRUTH

DISCOVER THE TRUTH

For this spell, you will need the following:
- Seven white candles
- Pin
- Picture of the person deceiving you
- Matches
- Waxing moon

Casting directions:
1. Hold up the candles and carve the name of the person you want the truth from. Also, carve the questions that you want answers to into the candles.
2. Light the candles one at a time and focus on the picture that you have up of the person. Visualize them

before you, and do not let their image disappear out of your focus. As you visualize them and put energy into the questions, you need to chant three times in succession:

Truth I seek.

Tell me no lies.

Questions answered.

No secrets shall you hide.

3. Once you are done, allow the candle to burn out. Repeat this action with the other six candles that you have remaining. It takes a lot of energy and concentration, which is why I recommend doing this during the waxing moon as your energy is in abundance here. You can stretch this spell into seven days and do one candle per night, leading up to the full moon if you like. As the weeks go on, once your spell is complete, you will discover all the answers to your questions.

DECIPHER THOUGHTS

For this spell, you will need the following:
- Picture of the person
- Bit of dried rosemary
- Flameproof dish
- A small piece of paper
- White candle

Casting directions:

1. Cast your circle and light your white candle. Charge the candle with what you intend to find from the person. As you hold it and transfer energy into it, focus on truth and mental illumination. If you do not have a picture of the person, hold on to a strong mental picture and visualize them in front of you.

2. On a piece of paper, you need to write down: "I wish that what this person thinks of me will be revealed in my dreams." Fold the rosemary into the paper so that it is tightly bound, and then carefully light the paper with the candle flame. Put it in the flameproof dish, and as the paper burns, visualize the person's face in front of you and focus intently on what you want. Speak the following chant:

With dreamer's eyes, I seek to see

What this person thinks of me.

Be it good or be it ill,

Reveal to me as is my will.

3. Once the rosemary and paper stop burning, snuff out the candle. You will receive the answer to your question in your dreams. If you want to ensure you find out all the think of you, move the candle to your room and sleep next to the burning candle until the candle burns itself out.

COMPELLING THE TRUTH

For this spell, you will need the following:

- Purple candle
- Matches

Casting directions:

1. If someone has given you cause for concern or you are unsure of their intentions or if they have told you the truth, you need to get a purple candle and anoint it in sage oil.

2. Write the person you think is being untruthful onto a piece of paper nine times in a row. Write your own

name over the liar's name nine times as well. You need to place the paper underneath the purple candle and allow that candle to burn for seven days. So burn the candle for an hour each night. Each night that you light the candle, you should call their name out loud and say: "I compel you to tell me the truth!"

3. On the seventh night that the candle burns, wrap the leftover candle wax inside the paper and throw it into a running source of water like a stream or river. He or she will be compelled to tell the truth then and may confess to many lies, or perhaps they were being honest with you. Either way, you will find out the truth.

CLEAR CONFUSION AWAY

This spell relies on you color coding your feelings. For your reference, here is a list so you can pick your candle color to do the spell correctly:

- Blue—calm
- Red—love
- Orange—jealousy
- Yellow—happy
- Purple—stressed

- White—hopeless
- Teal—loss
- Gray—lonely
- Black—satisfied
- Green—lively
- Magenta—sick
- Steel Blue—sadness

For this spell, you will need the following:

- Memories
- 3 candles that represent your feelings

Casting directions:

1. You need to pick the three candle colors that represent emotions that are confusing you. Once you have these candles picked, you need to set them up at your altar. This is very important, so make sure your altar is ready for your spell casting and rituals.

2. Light your candles before you go to sleep and focus on the energy of recovery. Whenever you go to sleep or need to take a nap, play through all your memories as you are falling asleep. Everything and anything you can remember will help you with this spell.

3. Once you fall asleep, you will dream about the answer or about the way to solve your confusion. If you do not get it when you wake up from your dream, think about it. Sometimes we lose dreams as we wake up, so a dream journal that you write in when you wake up can help you keep track of what your dreams are telling you. It might take a while to understand because your brain has a weird way of presenting things and ideas to you, but keep writing your dreams down, and you will be able to decipher them.

TRUE IDENTITIES

For this spell, you will need the following:

- A picture of the person you wish to have their identity made known
- A black candle
- A container that is flameproof

Casting directions:

1. Light the black candle on your altar with the picture next to it. Say the following chant:

    The face you show is not yours.

    This is now to show who you truly are.

> *Let others see the person you pretend to be*
>
> *That I know and see.*
>
> *No more lies shall leave your lips.*
>
> *Only truth now when you speak.*
>
> *You cannot hide, for we can see*
>
> *Your true face for the world to see.*
>
> *On the gods and goddesses, I command this.*
>
> *This is my will and power. So might it be!*

2. Grab the picture and set it on fire with the candle flame. Place it in the container as it burns, and when it is all ash, take the container outside and let the wind blow the ashes away. Snuff the candle out, and thank the gods and goddesses for their help in revealing the deceiver's identity.

SPELLS OF FERTILITY

ENHANCE YOUR FERTILITY

For this spell, you will need the following:

- One avocado
- One egg
- Twine or rope

Casting directions:

1. In your garden, find an appropriate place to dig a small hole that you can bury the avocado in. Once you have dug the hole, go and cut the avocado in half. You simply roll the knife around the avocado and twist it to separate the pieces.

2. Remove and put aside the seed from the middle of the fruit. Crack the egg open and take the yoke out. Do not break the yoke. If you do, then you need to get a new egg.

3. Place the egg yolk into the center of half the other avocado side. Close the avocado pieces together with the yolk still inside, and secure the fruit together by wrapping the avocado in the twine and knotting it up.

The avocado will symbolize your womb, and the egg symbolizes the life you want to grow inside your womb. Place the avocado and egg piece into the hole that you dug earlier and bury it.

4. Sit in front of your altar and meditate once you have buried the fruit. Focus positive energy toward your womb, and visualize life growing. You can burn white candles to symbolize positivity at your altar as well while you meditate.

BLESSINGS BY DEMETER

Demeter is the goddess of the earth, the harvest, and fertility. For the purpose of this spell, we will invoke her blessings so that she can bless the fertility of a woman's womb. However, if you are a person with a green thumb, you can also use this spell to ensure your crops turn out amazing!

For this spell, you will need the following:

- One green candle
- One A4 picture of a cornucopia
- One small sheaf of wheat
- One bunch of grapes
- One apple
- Two plums

- One orange
- One spade
- One bowl

Casting directions:

1. Place your green candle on your altar and light it. Green is used to represent prosperity, nature, wealth, and luck within this spell.

2. The picture of the cornucopia can be printed from Google, or you can take a picture of a cornucopia you may have physically. You could also find it on your phone, but you need to print the picture out. Or if you like, you could even draw the cornucopia if you have realistic drawing skills. The cornucopia is one of Demeter's symbols, and it represents abundance and nourishment.

3. Place the picture of the cornucopia in front of the lit green candle. Once the picture of the cornucopia is up, grab your mini sheaf of wheat and place it on the left-hand side of your picture. It is crucial for it to be on the left side. Place your grapes, orange, apple, and plums on the right side of the image. Chant once everything is in place:

   Demeter, Demeter!

> *Great goddess of the harvest, forests, and earth,*
>
> *I call you to kindly ask your blessing on fertility.*
>
> *I possess the image of the cornucopia in your honor to represent abundance.*
>
> *I possess a sheaf of wheat in your honor to represent fertility.*
>
> *I possess a green candle in your honor to represent prosperity, the earth, and luck.*
>
> *Oh, Demeter, I request of you to bless this sheaf of wheat, and when I scatter the ashes of it upon my tummy, may my womb be blessed for abundance equally. With your blessing, let my womb thrive!*
>
> *In return, I offer you the fruit and my eternal thanks.*

4. Now that your incantation is over, place the sheaf of wheat in your fireproof bowl. Drip some of the candle wax onto the wheat, but do not overly cover it.

5. Next, set the wheat on fire using the green candle. Make sure all the wheat has turned into ashes once

the flame has burned out. Do not leave any wheat unburned.

6. Walk outside with the ashes, fruit, and the spade. With your spade, you need to dig a hole to place all the fruit in. Cover the hole up once your offering has been delivered into the hole, and offer this thanks to Demeter:

> *Demeter, I offer this fruit to you in thanks for your blessing.*

As soon as you feel you have been acknowledged, you can move away from this area. If you do not feel like you have been heard yet, you can repeat your chant again a little slower than the first time you said it.

7. Make sure the ashes are 100 percent cool before you take them and scatter them on your belly. Place your hands on your stomach and close your eyes as you meditate positive energy into your womb. As you focus on your womb, you need to claim your blessing:

> *Let the ashes that Demeter has kindly blessed ensure abundance, survival, and that my womb may thrive. I thank Demeter, and she is in my favor eternally.*

CONCLUSION

This guide is meant as your first wade into Wicca. In other words, you are merely dipping your toes into the possibilities that Wicca can provide to you.

I know it can seem confusing, but it is also exhilarating, amazing, and rewarding. If you are left over with some questions, I am going to just quickly address some frequently asked questions about Wicca before I turn you lose to practicing your magic!

Do all witches practice their magic with the same rituals?

Not at all! Your relationship with Wicca is your own personal one. As you become more comfortable with rituals, charms, and spell casting, you will be writing your own grimoires! Each witch might practice in their own way, but we all have lots we can learn from one another. This book is just a starting point for you as a beginner in Wicca!

Are you sure witchcraft and Wicca are not a cult?

I am positive! There is nothing remotely cult-like in the religion that is Wicca. Those misconceptions are based on the ideas that you see presented in the media. They do not reflect the realities of what Wicca really is. You are still a free-thinking individual if you practice Wicca—cults do not practice free-thinking ideology.

Do witches worship the devil?

This is another misconception that has worsened in recent years due to some popular television shows. Witches and Wiccans do not worship the devil. Remember rule number one? Do no harm. Wiccans believe that there is a powerful entity in the world that can take on many different forms and present itself as different deities.

Can only women be witches?

I am so glad you asked this! Not at all! Males or females can be witches. In Wicca, we do not use the term *warlock* as this is insulting since warlock means oath-breaker. So regardless of your gender, if you believe and you practice Wicca, then you are a witch! Is that not just great?

This book is intended as a guide for you to start your path and journey into the Wiccan world. Through this book, we explored a lot and covered a lot of ground, so before I say goodbye, I want to make sure that you remember the key points about Wicca.

Anyone can be Wiccan; you just need to believe in magic, have faith in your abilities, and believe there is a connection between you and the spiritual world that resides with us.

Wiccan religion is not a cult. We are not devil worshippers, and we do not intend harm to other people. We believe in free will. We believe it is our responsibility not to hurt anyone. We also believe that what we put out into this universe, we will get back times three.

Yes, there are bad Wiccans and witchcraft practices. Does this represent Wicca as a whole? No, it does not. Just as there are bad people that exist in all corners of the world, Wicca is no exception. The best that you can do is to obey the rules, respect your relationship with Mother Earth, and not fall into black magic.

Magic is a beautiful tool that you can use to make your life easier, as well as your family's life. It can even protect those that you love. Sometimes, it is as simple as your belief and meditation. Not every spell needs to be elaborate or intricate. You can create your own spells once you get comfortable in your relationship with witchcraft.

You have learned the basics of spell casting in this guide, and they are spells that range from good luck to fertility and. There are even spells about finding out the truth from those that you love. You need to remember that you cannot infringe upon a person's free will. You can ask the gods to reveal a truth to you, but you cannot force a person to love you or do your bidding. This is wrong and in direct violation of the rules that Wiccans live by.

You do not have to grow up in Wicca religion to be a Wiccan. Like any other faith, you can convert if you believe. There are several ways that you can practice Wicca as well. You can practice it on your own, or you can join a coven.

The spells in this book all focus on magic that you will practice on your own.

Yes, you will use a lot of candles and matches. Your altar is your holy space of spiritual recharge. It is important that you set one up in your home to strengthen your connection. I suggest that as you are just starting out with Wicca, you should practice transferring energy and meditating.

Meditation and energy transference will be your two best friends through any spell you cast with Wicca. You will probably gain an entirely new appreciation for the way that your mind works.

I am so proud of you for making it through this introduction to Wicca and the spells to follow! I hope this is a guide that you can cherish and reference back to throughout different periods of your Wicca journey. Do not hesitate to research, reach out to other Wiccans, and practice! Practice! Practice!

I will leave you with two thoughts:

The first is that it can be easy to get tempted when you are first introduced to Wicca. When someone slights you, getting revenge can seem easy, and we can often put it out into the world before we think about it. But I urge you to stop and think. Keep the rule of three in mind. Whatever you do to that person will come back onto you and times three. So remain positive even in the face of your adversaries. I have faith in you.

The second thought is to have fun and cherish your relationship with nature! There is so much that Wicca can teach you. It teaches me more every day too! We are in this journey together, and I know that you are on the right path to becoming a witch that just glows with good energy!

REFERENCES

Fields, K. (2019). *Altar Set-Up for Beginners and Witches on a Budget.* Retrieved from https://exemplore.com/wicca-witchcraft/Wiccan-Altar-Set-Up-For-Beginner-Wiccans-or-Wiccans-on-a-Budget.

Fox, S. (2019). *Introduction to the Wiccan Religion and Contemporary Paganism.* Retrieved from https://www.circlesanctuary.org/index.php/about-paganism/introduction-to-the-wiccan-religion-and-contemporary-paganism.

Spells - Real Magic Spells. (2019). Retrieved from https://www.spellsofmagic.com/spells.html.

The Dangers of Love Spells. (2019). Retrieved from http://www.wiccanuniverse.com/blog/the-dangers-of-love-spells/.

What is Wicca?. (2003). Retrieved from https://wicca.com/celtic/wicca/wicca.htm

Witchcraft, Wicca and Paganism FAQ. (2019). Retrieved from https://wicca.com/celtic/wicca/faq.htm.

www.ingramcontent.com/pod-product-compliance
Lightning Source LLC
Chambersburg PA
CBHW030112100526
44591CB00009B/373